The Scrolls
Illuminated

An illuminating presentation of
Solomon's Song of Songs
Ruth
Lamentations
Ecclesiastes
& Esther

From the Holy Bible, English Standard Version 2001

With illustrations of Australian nature

by Fiona Pfennigwerth

Artist's Preface to the Manuscripts

My aim is to present the books of *The Song of Solomon*, *Ruth*, *Lamentations*, *Ecclesiastes* and *Esther* from the Hebrew Bible as an invitation to you to read, explore and respond to them. I hope you find them readable, contemporary yet timeless, whose meanings are made more accessible to you through the visual means of layout and drawings. I hope you find them decorative yet contemplative.

For each book I chose a separate Australian habitat that I thought somehow reflects it. The happy colours of spring in the country for *The Song of Solomon* – the earthiness of leaf litter, the sensuous-shaped trees and fragrant flowers, and the curvilinear hardenbergia vine like a melody line. For *Ruth*, the clear primary colours represent both harvest and the tone of its story and characters. The bleached pain of bushfire damage reflects *Lamentations*. The ebb and flow of life on the tidal mudflats of *Ecclesiastes* are sketched in its muted and bright tones of cloud and sun, and life and death. The rainforest's rank lushness suggests the ornate opulence of *Esther's* palace, in the style of Oscar Wilde rather than *Ruth's* Jane Austen.

The illustrations that form the border designs are my own visual response to the books, after careful, firsthand interaction with them, later enriched by others' more expert insight. Through the drawings and layout I suggest the major themes and literary devices that I perceive (or conjecture!) to assist your own exploration of these works. I do not want to retell the stories (and thus confine them) by depicting figures or historical places. Rather, I wish to extend their message by the timeless images of a natural habitat which is "at the uttermost end of the earth" to that in which they were originally conceived.

At the end of each manuscript is a brief explanation of my design, which I explore more fully in my studies in Natural History Illustration at the University of Newcastle, Australia – my dissertation for Honours for *The Song*, and PhD exegesis for the other four books.

These five books form a set in the Hebrew Scriptures (the Christian Old Testament) known as *The Scrolls*. They are read at five of the annual Jewish festivals. The first and last celebrate deliverance: *The Song* at Passover, and *Esther* at Purim. *Ruth* is read at the Feast of Weeks, which is associated with the barley harvest, and celebrates God's blessings and the giving of the law to Israel. *Lamentations* is read on the Ninth of Ab, which remembers the fall of Jerusalem and Jewish tragedies ever since. *Ecclesiastes* is read at the Feast of Tabernacles, which celebrates the end of the agricultural year and recalls the journey through the wilderness from Egypt to the Promised Land. It acknowledges God's providence in the changes and chances of this fleeting life. A friend of mine calls them "passages for rites", as they could similarly be read in response to more familiar milestones: marriage (*The Song*) and grief (*Lamentations*); coming of age or graduation for someone on the threshold of adulthood (*Ecclesiastes*); and thanksgiving for provision (*Ruth*) and rescue (*Esther*).

From their various perspectives these books give us glimpses into the mysterious nature, firstly of God: his love and generosity, his anger at his people's rejection and his desire for their restoration, his hidden workings and his universal concern. And secondly, into the common experiences and dilemmas of our lives – romance and love, birth and death, and finding meaning and values in our work and social and political relationships. The texts are subtle and sophisticated, and beautifully and carefully crafted.

I chose the English Standard Version of the Bible, because its goals are well suited to my project. Its Preface says it "seeks as far as possible to capture the precise wording of the original text and the personal style of each Bible writer... Thus it seeks to be transparent to the original text, letting the reader see as directly as possible the structure and meaning of the original" (ESV 2001:vii).

My initial work in understanding each text was to read it carefully both individually and in a group, using the "manuscript discovery" method. I was introduced to this literary approach at Christian tertiary student conferences in the late 1970s. In this method, the whole text being studied is set out as a "manuscript" to reflect its original format. That is, it is printed without editorial imports such as chapter or verse references or sub-headings. Page and line numbers are shown, and enough space around the text to allow notes. Group members are given this "manuscript" to "discover", reading it individually and then discussing their findings. It is studied as a whole work, as readers explore its structure, themes and possible purposes. The process begins by members individually reading straight through the text to gain a first impression of it, a second reading to build on that, and many more to gain deeper and deeper understanding, similar to an archaeological dig from the surface down. At each stage, findings are discussed in the group. By the end of the study, the manuscripts have been scribbled over, highlighted in multi-colours as themes are traced throughout, and structures suggested. In this way, discoveries are "owned", and the text becomes a known friend. I recommend you try this method for yourself on another short book, purchasing your own digital copy of the Bible.

As my ideas evolved, I reformatted the text into paragraphs and stanzas, sections and headings. From this intensive study, ideas for the visuals developed, which in turn I happily researched through field trips to all the diverse and beautiful locations I had chosen, and visits to Botanic Gardens, museums and zoos. Working on the drawings led to further study of the texts – and thus the process cycled through to the stage that this book represents, though it could have followed a number of different directions to a different result.

I seek to reflect the beauty I found in both my own natural environment and the texts I studied. My work is not a Natural History text, nor a commentary. For the latter I recommend Barry Webb's *Five Festal Garments: Christian Reflections on the Song of Songs, Ruth, Lamentations, Ecclesiastes and Esther* (New Studies in Biblical Theology 10, Leicester: InterVarsity Press 2000), or more briefly, William Dumbrell's *The Faith of Israel: a Theological Survey of the Old Testament* (Grand Rapids: Baker Academic 2002). Nor is it a literary guide. For that I recommend Leland Ryken's *How to read the Bible as literature... and get more out of it* (Grand Rapids: Zondervan 1984) or *Words of Delight: A Literary Introduction to the Bible* (Grand Rapids: Baker 1992). I also recommend A Complete Literary Guide to the Bible (Tremper Longman III, Grand Rapids: Zondervan 1993), and *The Literary Guide to the Bible* (Edited by Robert Alter and Frank Kermode, London: Collins 1987). But above all, I recommend you firstly simply read each book, and let its words and artistry enthral you.

The
Song
of
Songs,
which is
Solomon's

et him kiss me

with the kisses of his mouth!
For your love is better than wine;
    your anointing oils are fragrant;
your name is oil poured out;
    therefore virgins love you.
Draw me after you; let us run.
    The king has brought me into his chambers.

We will exult and rejoice in you;
    we will extol your love more than wine.

Rightly do they love you.
I am very dark, but lovely,
    O daughters of Jerusalem,
like the tents of Kedar,
    like the curtains of Solomon.

Do not gaze at me because I am dark,
    because the sun has looked upon me.
My mother's sons were angry with me;
    they made me keeper of the vineyards,
    but my own vineyard I have not kept!

Tell me, you whom my soul loves,
    where you pasture your flock,
    where you make it lie down at noon;
for why should I be like one who veils herself
    beside the flocks of your companions?

If you do not know, O most beautiful among women,
follow in the tracks of the flock,
    and pasture your young goats
    beside the shepherds' tents.

I compare you, my love,
    to a mare among Pharaoh's chariots.
Your cheeks are lovely with ornaments,
    your neck with strings of jewels.

**We will make for you
ornaments of gold,
  studded with silver.**

While the king was on his couch,
  my nard gave forth its fragrance.
My beloved is to me a sachet of myrrh
  that lies between my breasts.
My beloved is to me a cluster of henna blossoms
  in the vineyards of Engedi.

*Behold, you are beautiful, my love;
  behold, you are beautiful;
    your eyes are doves.*

Behold, you are beautiful, my beloved, truly delightful.
Our couch is green;

*the beams of our house are cedar;
  our rafters are pine.*

I am a rose of Sharon,
  a lily of the valleys.

*As a lily among brambles,
  so is my love among the young women.*

As an apple tree among the trees of the forest,
  so is my beloved among the young men.
With great delight I sat in his shadow,
  and his fruit was sweet to my taste,
He brought me to the house of wine,
  and his banner over me was love.
Sustain me with raisins;
  refresh me with apples,
    for I am sick with love.

His left hand is under my head,
  and his right hand embraces me!

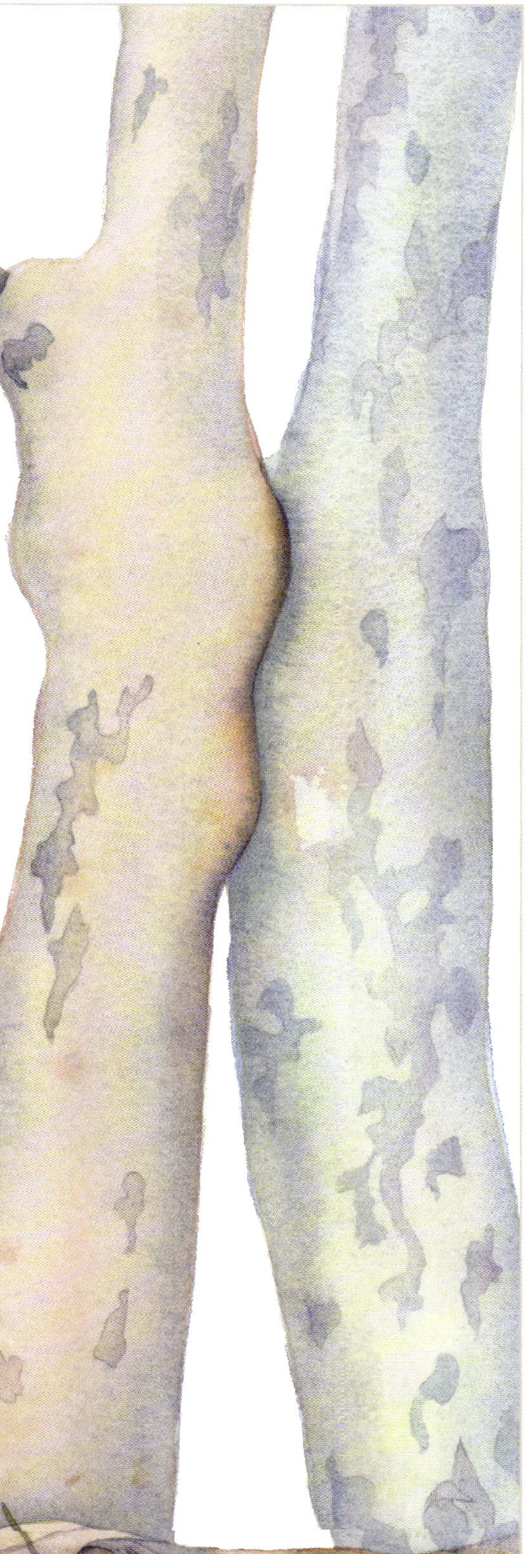

I put you on oath,
O daughters of Jerusalem,
by the gazelles or the does of the field,
that you not stir up or awaken love
until it pleases.

The voice of my beloved!

Behold, he comes,
leaping over the mountains,
   bounding over the hills.
My beloved is like a gazelle or a young stag.
Behold, there he stands behind our wall,
gazing through the windows,
   looking through the lattice.

My beloved speaks and says to me:
"Arise, my love, my beautiful one, and come away,
for behold, the winter is past;
   the rain is over and gone.
The flowers appear on the earth,
   the time of singing has come,
and the voice of the turtledove is heard in our land.
The fig tree ripens its figs,
   and the vines are in blossom;
   they give forth fragrance.
Arise, my love, my beautiful one, and come away".

O my dove, in the clefts of the rock,
   in the crannies of the cliff,
let me see your face,
   let me hear your voice,
for your voice is sweet, and your face is lovely.

Catch the foxes for us,
   the little foxes that spoil the vineyards,
   for our vineyards are in blossom.

My beloved is mine, and I am his;
   he grazes among the lilies.

Until the day breathes
   and the shadows flee,
turn, my beloved, be like a gazelle
   or a young stag on cleft mountains.

On my bed by night

I sought him whom my soul loves;
　　I sought him, but found him not.

I will rise now and go about the city,
　　in the streets and in the squares;
I will seek him whom my soul loves.
　　I sought him, but found him not.

The watchmen found me as they went about in the city.
"Have you seen him whom my soul loves?"
Scarcely had I passed them when I found him whom my soul loves.
I held him, and would not let him go
　　until I had brought him into my mother's house,
　　and into the chamber of her who conceived me.

I put you on oath, O daughters of Jerusalem,
　　by the gazelles or the does of the field,
that you not stir up or awaken love until it pleases.

What is that coming up from the wilderness

　　like columns of smoke,
perfumed with myrrh and frankincense,
　　with all the fragrant powders of a merchant?
Behold, it is the litter of Solomon!
Around it are sixty mighty men,
　　some of the mighty men of Israel,
all of them wearing swords and expert in war,
each with his sword at his thigh, against terror by night.
King Solomon made himself a carriage
　　from the wood of Lebanon.
He made its posts of silver,
　　its back of gold, its seat of purple;
its interior was inlaid with love
　　by the daughters of Jerusalem.
Go out, O daughters of Zion,
　　and look upon King Solomon,
with the crown with which his mother crowned him
　　on the day of his wedding,
　　on the day of the gladness of his heart.

Behold
you are beautiful, my love

behold, you are beautiful!

Your eyes are doves
   behind your veil.
Your hair is like a flock of goats
   leaping down the slopes of Gilead.
Your teeth are like a flock of shorn ewes
   that have come up from the washing,
all of which bear twins,
   and not one among them has lost its young.
Your lips are like a scarlet thread,
   and your mouth is lovely.
Your cheeks are like halves of a pomegranate
   behind your veil.
Your neck is like the tower of David,
   built in rows of stone;
on it hang a thousand shields,
   all of them shields of warriors.
Your two breasts are like two fawns,
   twins of a gazelle,
   that graze among the lilies.

Until the day breathes
   and the shadows flee,
I will go away to the mountain of myrrh
   and the hill of frankincense.

You are altogether beautiful, my love;
   there is no flaw in you.

ome with me

from Lebanon, my bride;
   come with me from Lebanon.
Depart from the peak of Amana,
   from the peak of Senir and Hermon,
from the dens of lions, from the mountains of leopards.

You have captivated my heart, my sister, my bride;
   you have captivated my heart with one glance of your eyes,
   with one jewel of your necklace.
How beautiful is your love, my sister, my bride!
   How much better is your love than wine,
   and the fragrance of your oils than any spice!
Your lips drip nectar, my bride;
   honey and milk are under your tongue;
   the fragrance of your garments is like the fragrance of Lebanon.

A garden locked is my sister, my bride,
   a spring locked, a fountain sealed.
Your shoots are an orchard of pomegranates with all choicest fruits,
   henna with nard,
nard and saffron, calamus and cinnamon,
   with all trees of frankincense,
myrrh and aloes, with all chief spices-
a garden fountain, a well of living water,
   and flowing streams from Lebanon.

Awake, O north wind,
   and come, O south wind!
Blow upon my garden,
   let its spices flow.
Let my beloved come to his garden,
   and eat its choicest fruits.

I came to my garden, my sister, my bride,
I gathered my myrrh with my spice,
I ate my honeycomb with my honey,
I drank my wine with my milk.

**Eat, friends, drink,
   and be drunk with love!**

A sound! My beloved is knocking.
"Open to me, my sister, my love,
    my dove, my perfect one,
for my head is wet with dew,
    my locks with the drops of the night."
I had put off my garment;
    how could I put it on?
I had bathed my feet;
    how could I soil them?
My beloved put his hand to the latch,
    and my heart was thrilled within me.
I arose to open to my beloved,
    and my hands dripped with myrrh,
my fingers with liquid myrrh,
    on the handles of the bolt.
I opened to my beloved,
    but my beloved had turned and gone.
My soul failed me when he spoke.
I sought him, but found him not;
    I called him, but he gave no answer.
The watchmen found me
    as they went about in the city;
they beat me, they bruised me,
    they took away my veil,
    those watchmen of the walls.
I put you on oath, O daughters of Jerusalem,
    if you find my beloved,
that you tell him
    I am sick with love.

What is your beloved more than another beloved,
    O most beautiful among women?
What is your beloved more than another beloved,
    that you thus adjure us?

My beloved is radiant and ruddy,
    distinguished among ten thousand.
His head is the finest gold;
    his locks are wavy, black as a raven.
His eyes are like doves
    beside streams of water,
bathed in milk, sitting beside a full pool.
His cheeks are like beds of spices,
    mounds of sweet-smelling herbs.
His lips are lilies,
    dripping liquid myrrh.
His arms are rods of gold,
    set with jewels.
His body is polished ivory,
    bedecked with lapis lazuli.[1]
His legs are alabaster columns,
    set on bases of gold.
His appearance is like Lebanon,
    choice as the cedars.
His mouth is most sweet,
    and he is altogether desirable.
This is my beloved and this is my friend,
    O daughters of Jerusalem.

Where has your beloved gone,
    O most beautiful among women?
Where has your beloved turned,
    that we may seek him with you?

My beloved has gone down to his garden
    to the beds of spices,
to graze in the gardens
    and to gather lilies.

I am my beloved's and my beloved is mine;
    he grazes among the lilies.

ou are beautiful as Tirzah, my love,

lovely as Jerusalem,
 awesome as an army with banners.
Turn away your eyes from me,
 for they overwhelm me –
Your hair is like a flock of goats
 leaping down the slopes of Gilead.
Your teeth are like a flock of ewes
 that have come up from the washing;
all of them bear twins;
 not one among them has lost its young.
Your cheeks are like halves of a pomegranate behind your veil.
There are sixty queens and eighty concubines,
 and virgins without number.
My dove, my perfect one, is the only one,
 the only one of her mother,
 pure to her who bore her.
The young women saw her and called her blessed;
 the queens and concubines also, and they praised her.

**Who is this who looks down like the dawn,
 beautiful as the moon, bright as the sun,
 awesome as an army with banners?**

I went down to the nut orchard
 to look at the blossoms of the valley,
to see whether the vines had budded,
 whether the pomegranates were in bloom.
Before I was aware, my desire set me
 among the chariots of Ammi-Nadib.[(2)]

Song of Songs 6:4-12

17

Return return, O Shulammite

return, return, that we may look upon you.

Why should you look upon the Shulammite,
  as upon a dance of Mahanaim? [3]

How beautiful are your feet in sandals, O noble daughter!
Your rounded thighs are like jewels,
  the work of a master hand.
Your navel is a rounded bowl
  that never lacks mixed wine.
Your belly is a heap of wheat,
  encircled with lilies.
Your two breasts are like two fawns,
  twins of a gazelle.
Your neck is like an ivory tower.
Your eyes are pools in Heshbon,
  by the gate of Bath-rabbim.
Your nose is like a tower of Lebanon,
  which looks toward Damascus.
Your head crowns you like Carmel,
  and your flowing locks are like purple;
  a king is held captive in the tresses.
How beautiful and pleasant you are,
  O loved one, with all your delights!
Your stature is like a palm tree,
  and your breasts are like its clusters.
I say I will climb the palm tree
  and lay hold of its fruit.
Oh may your breasts be like
   clusters of the vine,
  and the scent of your breath like apples,
and your mouth like the best wine.

It goes down smoothly for my beloved,
  gliding over lips and teeth.

I am my beloved's,
  and his desire is for me.

Song of Songs 6:13-7:10

Come, my beloved,

let us go out into the fields
  and lodge among the henna plants;[4]
let us go out early to the vineyards
  and see whether the vines have budded,
whether the grape blossoms have opened
  and the pomegranates are in bloom.
There I will give you my love.
The mandrakes give forth fragrance,
  and beside our doors are all choice fruits,
new as well as old,
  which I have laid up for you, O my beloved.

Oh that you were like a brother to me
  who nursed at my mother's breasts!
If I found you outside, I would kiss you,
  and none would despise me.
I would lead you and bring you
  into the house of my mother--
  she who used to teach me.
I would give you spiced wine to drink,
  the juice of my pomegranate.

His left hand is under my head,
  and his right hand embraces me!

I put you on oath,
O daughters of Jerusalem,
that you not stir up
or awaken love
until it pleases.

Song of Songs 8.4·14

Who is that

leaning on her beloved?

Under the apple tree I awakened you.
There your mother was in labor with you;
*   there she who bore you was in labor.*

Set me as a seal upon your heart,
   as a seal upon your arm,

for love is strong as death,
**   jealousy is fierce as the grave.**
Its flashes are flashes of fire,
**   the very flame of the LORD.**
Many waters cannot quench love,
**   neither can floods drown it.**
If a man offered for love
**   all the wealth of his house,**
**   he would be utterly despised.**

We have a little sister,
**   and she has no breasts.**
What shall we do for our sister
**   on the day when she is spoken for?**
If she is a wall,
**   we will build on her a battlement of silver,**
but if she is a door,
**   we will enclose her with boards of cedar.**

I was a wall,   and my breasts were like towers;
then I was in his eyes as one who brings out[5] peace.[6]

Solomon had a vineyard at Baal-hamon;
   he let out the vineyard to keepers;
      each one was to bring for its fruit a thousand pieces of silver.
My vineyard, my very own, is before me;
   you, O Solomon, may have the thousand,
   and the keepers of the fruit two hundred.

O you who dwell in the gardens,
*   with companions listening for your voice;*
*   let me hear it.*

Make haste, my beloved
*   and be like a gazelle*
*   or a young stag*
*   on the mountains of spices.*

Explaining this Song manuscript

Changes of font in the text

Font changes indicate different voices singing their parts:

Regular	the woman
Italics	the man
Bold	the chorus
Bold italics	the poet

Phrases in colour are headings and in gold mark section breaks. The Charge and description of love are in purple.

Notes

(1)–(5) I have chosen the alternative translations footnoted in the ESV, as I understand they are closer to the original Hebrew. I am unsure of the meaning of the phrases in (2) and (3). In the ESV text, (2) reads "among the chariots of my kinsman, a prince"; (3) "a dance before two armies"; and (5) "finds" rather than "brings out".

(6) Hebrew *shalom*, meaning wholeness, peace, wellbeing.

The illustrations are mainly of flora found in the Sydney region

Title Page	*Hardenbergia violacea* in leaf litter
	This vine continues in the lower borders throughout the manuscript
Page 8-9	**Illustration** "Let him kiss me": Smooth-barked apple *Angophora costata* and Spotted gum *Corymbia maculata*
	Initial letter Australian white cedar, *Melia azedarach variety australasica*
	Border includes *Angophora* and *Corymbia* fruit and cedar flower
Page 10-11	**Illustration** "lily of the valley": Gymea lily *Doryanthes excelsa*
	Initial letter Early nancy *Anguillaria dioica* and Fringed lily *Thysanotus tuberosus*
	Border includes the Fringed lily, Flannel flower *Actinotus helianthi* and Early nancy
Page 12-13	**Illustration** "Restless": banded skipper *Cephrenes augiades*
	Initial letter Lillypilly *Syzygium crebinerve* and Scentless rosewood *Synoum glandulosum*
	Border includes lillypillies, Scentless rosewood and Sarsparilla *Smilax australis*
Page 14-15	**Initial letter** the fragrant Native frangipani *hymenosporum flavum*
	Illustration "Shalom": banded skipper on honey-scented *Cuttsia viburnea*
	Border includes flowers of *Oxylobium scandens*, Sarsparilla, Mountain kangaroo apple *Solanum linearfolium* and *Pittosporum rhombifolium* as well as flora from all other panels
Page 16-17	**Initial letter and border** as in Panel 3, with banded skipper
Page 18-19	**Initial letter** Flannel flower and Early nancy
	Illustration and border as in Panel 2
Page 20-21	**Illustration** "Under the apple tree I awakened you"
	Flora in **illustration, initial letter and border** as in Panel 1

Comment

The Song is a sensuous love lyric, in turn frivolous and serious, innocent and erotic, grandiose and anxious, coyly allusional and in-your-face. Revelling in the natural world, it resonates with images of the Garden of Eden (Genesis 2), the Promised Land "of milk and honey" (Exodus 3), and King Solomon, supreme symbol of wealth and wisdom. Along with the poet and chorus, we are eavesdropping into the intimate exchanges and musings of a couple in love. Many read it as an allegory of the love between God and his people.

I designed this manuscript according to my organization of the text – one of many possible interpretations. I see the book as one song of three movements (fast, slow, fast) akin to sonata form. It pivots on the central emotional climax of the couple's marriage from wooing to consummation, and moves toward a final thematic climax describing love, with a gentle closing coda.

First movement
> **Panel 1** Song 1 Introduction (duo and chorus)
>
> **Panel 2** The Charge (poet)
>
> > Song 2 (duo)

Second movement : Four Night Muses
> **Panel 3** Song 1 The woman's dream (solo)
>
> > Song 2 The man's meditation (solo)
>
> > > Pivot
> > > **Panel 4** The bridal (trio)
>
> **Panel 5** Song 3 The woman's dream (solo)
>
> > Song 4 The man's meditation (solo)

Third movement
> **Panel 6** Song 1 (duo and chorus)
>
> **Panel 7** The Charge (poet)
>
> > Song 2 Epilogue and coda (trio and chorus)

This form suggests symmetry at many levels, through repeated phrases and motifs. The thrice-made Charge divides the Introduction and Epilogue from the remainder, and splices the woman's dream into ones of anxiety and aggrandisement. The pivot splices both the second movement and the whole.

I have chosen flora that roughly equate to those mentioned in the text – small wildflowers, lilies, fragrances and lush-looking fruits. The leaf litter in the lower borders suggests the rural setting of the lovers, contrasting favourably to the palace of Solomon. It reminds me of Jesus' words, "Consider the lilies of the field... even Solomon in all his glory was not arrayed like one of these" (Matthew 6:28-9). The gold background of panels 3 and 5 suggest the lovers' inner worlds, and the background of the central panel is bridal white. The banded skipper symbolises the woman's unsettled state of mind in panels 3 and 5, and the rapture of the garden in panel 4.

Ruth

In the days when the judges ruled there was a famine in the land,

and a man of Bethlehem in Judah went to sojourn in the country of Moab, he and his wife and his two sons. The name of the man was Elimelech and the name of his wife Naomi, and the names of his two sons were Mahlon and Chilion. They were Ephrathites from Bethlehem in Judah. They went into the country of Moab and remained there. But Elimelech, the husband of Naomi, died, and she was left with her two sons. These took Moabite wives; the name of the one was Orpah and the name of the other Ruth. They lived there about ten years, and both Mahlon and Chilion died, so that the woman was left without her two sons and her husband.

Then she arose with her daughters-in-law to return from the country of Moab, for she had heard in the fields of Moab that the LORD had visited his people and given them food. So she set out from the place where she was with her two daughters-in-law, and they went on the way to return to the land of Judah.

But Naomi said to her two daughters-in-law,

"Go, return each of you to her mother's house. May the LORD deal kindly with you, as you have dealt with the dead and with me. The LORD grant that you may find rest, each of you in the house of her husband!"

Then she kissed them, and they lifted up their voices and wept.

And they said to her, "No, we will return with you to your people." But Naomi said, "Turn back, my daughters; why will you go with me? Have I yet sons in my womb that they may become your husbands? Turn back, my daughters; go your way, for I am too old to have a husband. If I should say I have hope, even if I should have a husband this night and should bear sons, would you therefore wait till they were grown? Would you therefore refrain from marrying? No, my daughters, for it is exceedingly bitter to me for your sake that the hand of the LORD has gone out against me." Then they lifted up their voices and wept again.

And Orpah kissed her mother-in-law, but Ruth clung to her. And she said, "See, your sister-in-law has gone back to her people and to her gods; return after your sister-in-law."

But Ruth said,

"Do not urge me to leave you or to return from following you. For where you go I will go, and where you lodge I will lodge. Your people shall be my people, and your God my God. Where you die I will die, and there will I be buried. May the LORD do so to me and more also if anything but death parts me from you."

And when Naomi saw that she was determined to go with her, she said no more. So the two of them went on until they came to Bethlehem.

And when they came to Bethlehem, the whole town was stirred because of them. And the women said, "Is this Naomi?" She said to them, "Do not call me Naomi; call me Mara, for the Almighty has dealt very bitterly with me. I went away full, and the LORD has brought me back empty. Why call me Naomi, when the LORD has testified against me and the Almighty has brought calamity upon me?"

So Naomi returned, and Ruth the Moabite her daughter-in-law with her, who returned from the country of Moab. And they came to Bethlehem *at the beginning of barley harvest.*

Now Naomi had a relative of her husband's, a worthy man of the clan of Elimelech, whose name was Boaz. And Ruth the Moabite said to Naomi,

"Let me go to the field and glean

among the ears of grain after him in whose sight I shall find favour." And she said to her, "Go, my daughter." So she set out and went and gleaned in the field after the reapers, and she happened to come to the part of the field belonging to Boaz, who was of the clan of Elimelech.

And **behold**, Boaz came from Bethlehem. And he said to the reapers, "The LORD be with you!" And they answered, "The LORD bless you." Then Boaz said to his young man who was in charge of the reapers, "Whose young woman is this?" And the servant who was in charge of the reapers answered, "She is the young Moabite woman, who came back with Naomi from the country of Moab. She said, 'Please let me glean and gather among the sheaves after the reapers.' So she came, and she has continued from early morning until now, except for a short rest."

Then Boaz said to Ruth, "Now, listen, my daughter, do not go to glean in another field or leave this one, but keep close to my young women. Let your eyes be on the field that they are reaping, and go after them. Have I not charged the young men not to touch you? And when you are thirsty, go to the vessels and drink what the young men have drawn."

Then she fell on her face, bowing to the ground, and said to him, "Why have I found favour in your eyes, that you should take notice of me, since I am a foreigner?" But Boaz answered her, "All that you have done for your mother-in-law since the death of your husband has been fully told to me, and how you left your father and mother and your native land and came to a people that you did not know before.

The LORD repay you for what you have done, and a full reward be given you by the LORD, the God of Israel, under whose wings you have come to take refuge!"

Then she said, "I have found favour in your eyes, my lord, for you have comforted me and spoken kindly to your servant, though I am not one of your servants."

And at mealtime Boaz said to her, "Come here and eat some bread and dip your morsel in the wine." So she sat beside the reapers, and he passed to her roasted grain. And she ate until she was satisfied, and she had some left over.

When she rose to glean, Boaz instructed his young men, saying, "Let her glean even among the sheaves, and do not reproach her. And also pull out some from the bundles for her and leave it for her to glean, and do not rebuke her."

So she gleaned in the field until evening. Then she beat out what she had gleaned, and it was about an ephah[1] of barley. And she took it up and went into the city.

Her mother-in-law saw what she had gleaned. She also brought out and gave her what food she had left over after being satisfied. And her mother-in-law said to her, "Where did you glean today? And where have you worked? Blessed be the man who took notice of you." So she told her mother-in-law with whom she had worked and said, "The man's name with whom I worked today is Boaz." And Naomi said to her daughter-in-law,

"May he be blessed by the LORD, whose kindness has not forsaken the living or the dead!"

Naomi also said to her, "The man is a close relative of ours, one of our redeemers." And Ruth the Moabite said, "Besides, he said to me, 'You shall keep close by my young men until they have finished all my harvest.'" And Naomi said to Ruth, her daughter-in-law, "It is good, my daughter, that you go out with his young women, lest in another field you be assaulted."

So she kept close to the young women of Boaz, gleaning until the end of the barley and wheat harvests. And she lived with her mother-in-law.

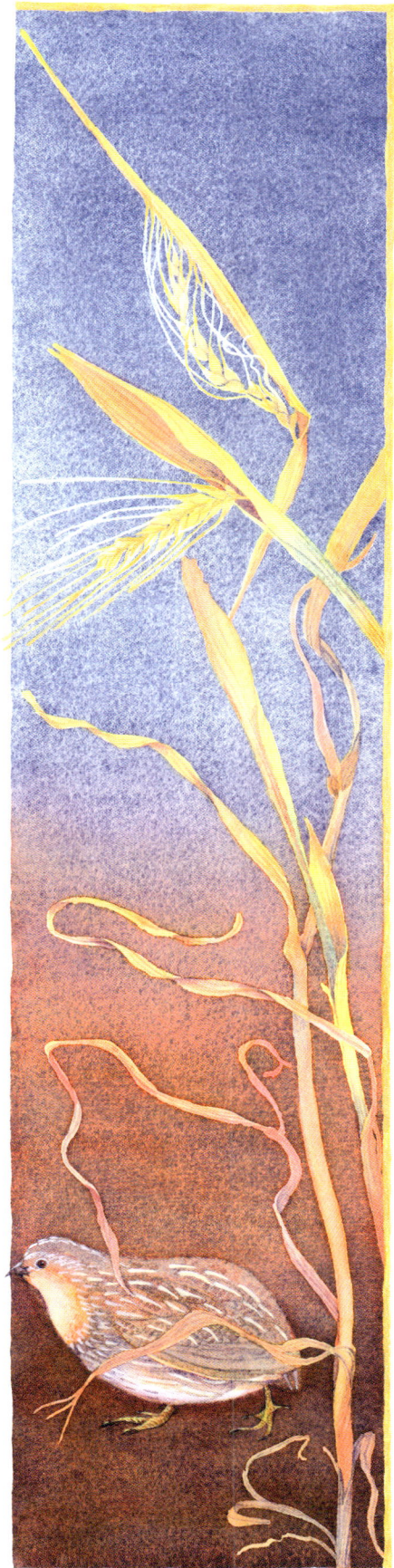

Then Naomi her mother-in-law said to her,

"My daughter, should I not seek rest for you, that it may be well with you?

Is not Boaz our relative, with whose young women you were? See, he is winnowing barley tonight at the threshing floor. Wash therefore and anoint yourself, and put on your cloak and go down to the threshing floor, but do not make yourself known to the man until he has finished eating and drinking. But when he lies down, observe the place where he lies. Then go and uncover his feet and lie down, and he will tell you what to do."

And she replied, "All that you say I will do."

So she went down to the threshing floor and did just as her mother-in-law had commanded her.

And when Boaz had eaten and drunk, and his heart was merry, he went to lie down at the end of the heap of grain. Then she came softly and uncovered his feet and lay down.

At midnight the man was startled and turned over, and **behold**, a woman lay at his feet!

He said, "Who are you?" And she answered, "I am Ruth, your servant. Spread your wings over your servant, for you are a redeemer."

And he said, "May you be blessed by the LORD, my daughter. You have made this last kindness greater than the first in that you have not gone after young men, whether poor or rich.

And now, my daughter, do not fear. I will do for you all that you ask, for all my fellow townsmen know that you are a worthy woman.

And now it is true that I am a redeemer. Yet there is a redeemer nearer than I. Remain tonight, and in the morning, if he will redeem you, good; let him do it. But if he is not willing to redeem you, then, as the LORD lives, I will redeem you. Lie down until the morning."

So she lay at his feet until the morning, but arose before one could recognize another. And he said, "Let it not be known that the woman came to the threshing floor."

And he said, "Bring the garment you are wearing and hold it out." So she held it, and he measured out six measures of barley and put it on her. Then she went into the city.

And when she came to her mother-in-law, she said, "How did you fare, my daughter?"

Then she told her all that the man had done for her, saying, "These six measures of barley he gave to me, for he said to me, 'You must not go back empty-handed to your mother-in-law.'"

She replied, "Wait, my daughter, until you learn how the matter turns out, for the man will not rest but will settle the matter today."

Now Boaz had gone up to the gate and sat down there.

And **behold**, the redeemer, of whom Boaz had spoken, came by. So Boaz said, "Turn aside, friend; sit down here." And he turned aside and sat down. And he took ten men of the elders of the city and said, "Sit down here." So they sat down.

Then he said to the redeemer, "Naomi, who has come back from the country of Moab, is selling the parcel of land that belonged to our relative Elimelech. So I thought I would tell you of it and say, 'Buy it in the presence of those sitting here and in the presence of the elders of my people.' If you will redeem it, redeem it. But if you will not, tell me, that I may know, for there is no one besides you to redeem it, and I come after you." And he said, "I will redeem it."

Then Boaz said, "The day you buy the field from the hand of Naomi, you also acquire Ruth the Moabite, the widow of the dead, in order to perpetuate the name of the dead in his inheritance."

Then the redeemer said, "I cannot redeem it for myself, lest I impair my own inheritance. Take my right of redemption yourself, for I cannot redeem it." Now this was the custom in former times in Israel concerning redeeming and exchanging: to confirm a transaction, the one drew off his sandal and gave it to the other, and this was the manner of attesting in Israel. So when the redeemer said to Boaz, "Buy it for yourself," he drew off his sandal.

Then Boaz said to the elders and all the people,

"You are witnesses this day that I have bought from the hand of Naomi all that belonged to Elimelech and all that belonged to Chilion and to Mahlon. Also Ruth the Moabite, the widow of Mahlon, I have bought to be my wife, to perpetuate the name of the dead in his inheritance, that the name of the dead may not be cut off from among his brothers and from the gate of his native place. You are witnesses this day."

Then all the people who were at the gate and the elders said, "We are witnesses.

"May the LORD make the woman, who is coming into your house, like Rachel and Leah, who together built up the house of Israel. May you act worthily in Ephrathah and be renowned in Bethlehem, and may your house be like the house of Perez, whom Tamar bore to Judah, because of the offspring that the LORD will give you by this young woman."

So Boaz took Ruth, and she became his wife. And he went in to her, and the LORD gave her conception, and she bore a son.

Then the women said to Naomi,

"Blessed be the LORD, who has not left you this day without a redeemer, and may his name be renowned in Israel! He shall be to you a restorer of life and a nourisher of your old age, for your daughter-in-law who loves you, who is more to you than seven sons, has given birth to him."

Then Naomi took the child and laid him on her lap and became his nurse.

And the women of the neighbourhood gave him a name, saying, "A son has been born to Naomi."

They named him Obed. He was the father of Jesse, the father of **David.**

Now these are the generations of Perez: Perez fathered Hezron, Hezron fathered Ram, Ram fathered Amminadab, Amminadab fathered Nahshon, Nahshon fathered Salmon, Salmon fathered Boaz, Boaz fathered Obed, Obed fathered Jesse, and Jesse fathered **David.**

Explaining this Ruth manuscript

Changes of font in the text

Emphases are in **bold**, including the word **behold**, which is a code word for pay attention

I use ***bold italics*** to begin a section (with decorative first letter) and to highlight the central pivot of the whole book and of each part (which are mostly blessings)

Note

(1) an ephah is about 22 litres

The illustrations are mostly of harvest in the New England Tablelands, New South Wales

Title Page	From famine to harvest and from bitter to pleasant, in covenant rainbow colours
Page 26-27	*Left* The bitter fruit of the Kangaroo apple, *Solanum aviculare*: "Call me bitter..."
	Withered kangaroo apple leaf: ten years of death
	Right Between famine and harvest, a barley seed sown
Page 28-29	*Left* Ripe barley, Dianella flower and feather of the Stubble Quail, *Coturnix pectoralis*
	Right Daytime harvest: barley and quail
Page 30-31	*Left* Study of a barley head and the pleasant Dianella fruit
	Right Night-time winnowing: barley and quail
Page 32-33	*Left* The pleasant fruits of the Kangaroo apple, *Solanum laciniatum* and Dianella
	Right Quail egg and feather, barley seed and pleasant fruits: ten generations of life
	Completion of the harvest

Barley was introduced to Australia early in European settlement; like Ruth, an alien in a new homeland. The progress of the barley crop mirrors Ruth's fortunes: she sows commitment between famine and the crop's maturity. She reaps a blessing in the centre of the harvest. She gathers in a promise of marriage – redemption and security (*rest*) for both herself and Naomi – at the in-gathering at the threshing floor. In the final chapter, she conceives and gives birth to Obed – a new planting and a new harvest. I sketched the barley harvest at *Bernleigh*, a property near Inverell in the New England region of New South Wales, and gleaned samples to draw back in the studio. I planted seeds in a pot, and sketched the plants as they grew.

An empty Naomi grieves bitterly in chapter 1, but at the end of chapter 2, the centre of the book, realises that God has not forsaken her. The story ends with her surrounded by friends and family, arms full of her new grandson. *Naomi* means *pleasant* and so I suggest her story by bitter fruits in panel 1, and dianella flowers in panel 2, anticipating the pleasant fruits in panels 3 and 4.

Boaz appears in chapter 2, a worthy man full of blessings. I symbolise him and his exchanges with Ruth with quail, a gentle bird common in barley-fields. His blessing at the centre of chapter 2 is echoed by Ruth's words at the centre of chapter 3, in which he calls her *worthy*. The chapter is full of innuendo, suggesting sexual tension, but also of words for "good" that suggest the alternative and more complete consummation. Thus chapters 2 and 3 are in parallel, which I show by motif and colour scheme. Chapter 4 contrasts and resolves the bereavement and vulnerable journey of chapter 1, which I suggest similarly.

Look at repeated words: *return* in chapter 1 (the same word in Hebrew as *repent*); *rest*; *kindness*; *blessing*; *good/well/better*; *worthy*; *favour visit*. Consider the echoes of *rest* and God's *loving-kindness* throughout the Scriptures. Look at the contrasts: full and empty; two daughters-in-law; two redeemers; two couples in relation to levirate marriage (see Deuteronomy 25), Boaz and Ruth and the first couple in the genealogy, Judah and Tamar (see Genesis 38).

It is a book about faithfulness kept with a generosity of heart, which I seek to convey in the paintings by layering the pure colours of cobalt blue deep, quinacridone red and aureolin and touches of gold. This is Moses' law kept in its true spirit, in contrast to the story's setting in the times when the judges judged. It is about God's character and presence seen in his visits and coincidences, and the foreshadowing of another baby born as king.

Lamentations

איכה

How lonely sits the city
that was full of people!
How like a widow has she become
she who was great among the nations!

She who was a princess among the provinces
   has become a slave.

She weeps bitterly in the night,
   with tears on her cheeks;
among all her lovers
   she has none to comfort her;
all her friends have dealt treacherously with her;
   they have become her enemies.

Judah has gone into exile because of affliction
   and hard servitude;
she dwells now among the nations,
   but finds no resting place;
her pursuers have all overtaken her
   in the midst of her distress.

The roads to Zion mourn,
   for none come to the festival;
all her gates are desolate;
   her priests groan;
her virgins have been afflicted,
   and she herself suffers bitterly.

Her foes have become the head;
   her enemies prosper,
because the LORD has afflicted her
   for the multitude of her transgressions;
her children have gone away,
   captives before the foe.

From the daughter of Zion
   all her majesty has departed.
Her princes have become like deer
   that find no pasture;
they fled without strength
   before the pursuer.

Jerusalem remembers
   in the days of her affliction and wandering
all the precious things
   that were hers from days of old.
When her people fell into the hand of the foe,
   and there was none to help her,
her foes gloated over her;
   they mocked at her downfall.

ח

ט

י

ל

מ

ס

Jerusalem sinned grievously;
  therefore she became filthy;
all who honoured her despise her,
  for they have seen her nakedness;
she herself groans
  and turns her face away.

Her uncleanness was in her skirts;
  she took no thought of her future;
therefore her fall is terrible;
  she has no comforter.
**O LORD, behold my affliction,
  for the enemy has triumphed!**

The enemy has stretched out his hands
  over all her precious things;
for she has seen the nations
  enter her sanctuary,
those whom you forbade
  to enter your congregation.

All her people groan
  as they search for bread;
they trade their treasures for food
  to revive their strength.
*Look, O LORD, and see,
  for I am despised.*

*Is it nothing to you,
all you who pass by?
  Look and see
if there is any sorrow like my sorrow,
  which was brought upon me,
which the LORD inflicted
  on the day of his fierce anger.*

*From on high he sent fire;
  into my bones he made it descend;
he spread a net for my feet;
  he turned me back;
he has left me stunned,
  faint all the day long.*

*My transgressions were bound into a yoke;
  by his hand they were fastened together;
they were set upon my neck;
  he caused my strength to fail;
the Lord gave me into the hands
  of those whom I cannot withstand.*

*The Lord rejected
  all my mighty men in my midst;
he summoned an assembly against me
  to crush my young men;
the Lord has trodden as in a winepress
  the virgin daughter of Judah.*

Lamentations 1·8-15

For these things I weep;
  my eyes flow with tears;
for a comforter is far from me,
  one to revive my spirit;
my children are desolate,
  for the enemy has prevailed.

Zion stretches out her hands,
  but there is none to comfort her;
the LORD has commanded against Jacob
  that his neighbours should be his foes;
Jerusalem has become
  a filthy thing among them.

The LORD is in the right,
  for I have rebelled against his word;
**but hear, all you peoples,
  and see my suffering;**
my young women and my young men
  have gone into captivity.

I called to my lovers,
  but they deceived me;
my priests and elders
  perished in the city,
while they sought food
  to revive their strength.

Look, O LORD, for I am in distress;
  my stomach churns;
my heart is wrung within me,
  because I have been very rebellious.
In the street the sword bereaves;
  in the house it is like death.

They heard my groaning,
  yet there is no one to comfort me.
All my enemies have heard of my trouble;
  they are glad that you have done it.
You have brought the day you announced;
  now let them be as I am.

**Let all their evildoing come before you,
  and deal with them
as you have dealt with me**
  because of all my transgressions;
for my groans are many,
  and my heart is faint.

How the Lord in his anger has set the daughter of Zion under a cloud!

He has cast down from heaven to earth
  the splendour of Israel;
he has not remembered his footstool
  in the day of his anger.

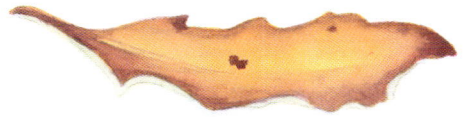

The Lord has swallowed up without mercy
  all the habitations of Jacob;
in his wrath he has broken down
  the strongholds of the daughter of Judah;
he has brought down to the ground in dishonour
  the kingdom and its rulers.

He has cut down in fierce anger
  all the might of Israel;
he has withdrawn from them his right hand
  in the face of the enemy;
he has burned like a flaming fire in Jacob,
  consuming all around.

He has bent his bow like an enemy,
  with his right hand set like a foe;
and he has killed all who were delightful
in our eyes
  in the tent of the daughter of Zion;
he has poured out his fury like fire.

The Lord has become like an enemy;
  he has swallowed up Israel;
he has swallowed up all its palaces;
  he has laid in ruins its strongholds,
and he has multiplied in the daughter of Judah
  mourning and lamentation.

He has laid waste his booth like a garden,
  laid in ruins his meeting place;
the LORD has made Zion forget
  festival and Sabbath,
and in his fierce indignation has spurned
king and priest.

The Lord has scorned his altar,
  disowned his sanctuary;
he has delivered into the hand of the enemy
  the walls of her palaces;
they raised a clamour in the house of the LORD
  as on the day of festival.

Lamentations 2:1-7

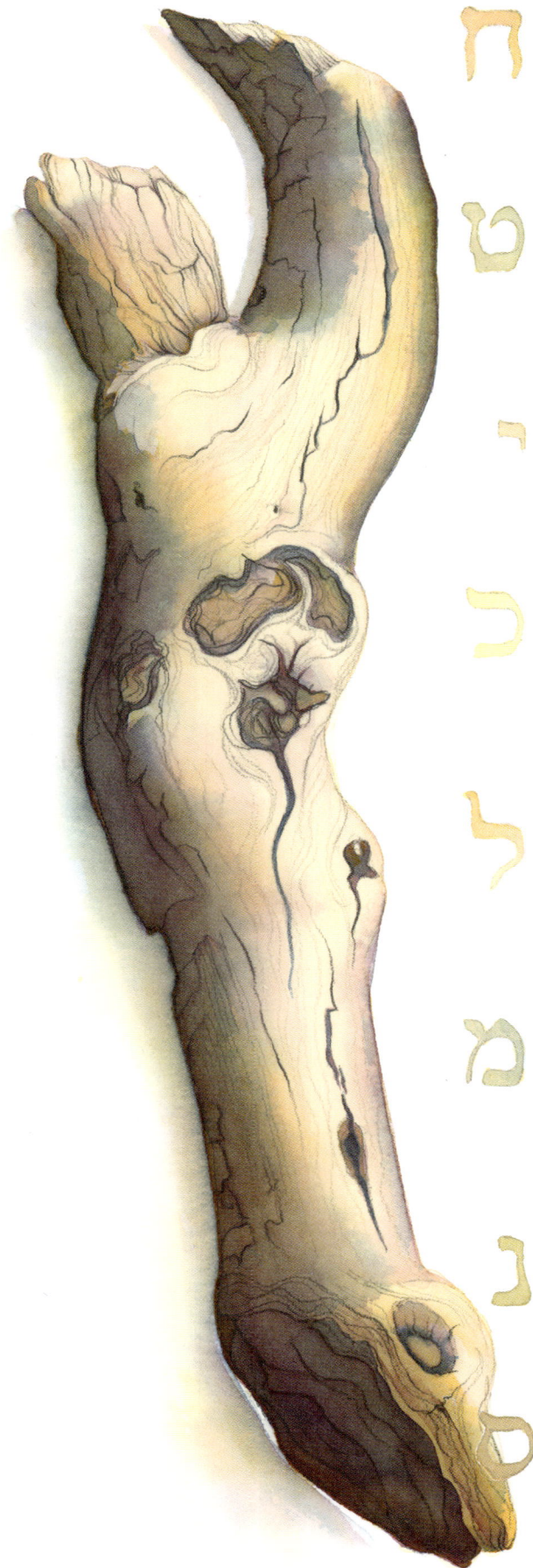

ח The LORD determined to lay in ruins
the wall of the daughter of Zion;
he stretched out the measuring line;
he did not restrain his hand from destroying;
he caused rampart and wall to lament;
they languished together.

ט Her gates have sunk into the ground;
he has ruined and broken her bars;
her king and princes are among the nations;
the law is no more,
and her prophets find
no vision from the LORD.

י The elders of the daughter of Zion
sit on the ground in silence;
they have thrown dust on their heads
and put on sackcloth;
the young women of Jerusalem
have bowed their heads to the ground.

כ *My eyes are spent with weeping;*
my stomach churns;
my bile is poured out to the ground
because of the destruction of the daughter of my people,
because infants and babies faint
in the streets of the city.

ל They cry to their mothers,
"Where is bread and wine?"
as they faint like a wounded man
in the streets of the city,
as their life is poured out
on their mothers' bosom.

מ What can I say for you,
to what compare you,
O daughter of Jerusalem?
What can I liken to you,
that I may comfort you,
O virgin daughter of Zion?
For your ruin is vast as the sea;
who can heal you?

נ Your prophets have seen for you
false and deceptive visions;
they have not exposed your iniquity
to restore your fortunes,
but have seen for you oracles
that are false and misleading.

ס All who pass along the way
clap their hands at you;
they hiss and wag their heads
at the daughter of Jerusalem;

"Is this the city that was called
    the perfection of beauty,
    the joy of all the earth?"

All your enemies
    rail against you;
they hiss, they gnash their teeth,
    they cry: "We have swallowed her!
Ah, this is the day we longed for;
    now we have it; we see it!"

The LORD has done what he purposed;
    he has carried out his word,
which he commanded long ago;
    he has thrown down without pity;
he has made the enemy rejoice over you
    and exalted the might of your foes.

Their heart cried to the Lord.
    O wall of the daughter of Zion,
let tears stream down like a torrent
    day and night!
Give yourself no rest,
    your eyes no respite!

Arise, cry out in the night,
    at the beginning of the night watches!
Pour out your heart like water
    before the presence of the Lord!
Lift your hands to him
    for the lives of your children,
who faint for hunger
    at the head of every street.

Look, O LORD, and see!
    With whom have you dealt thus?
Should women eat the fruit of their womb,
    the children of their tender care?
Should priest and prophet be killed
    in the sanctuary of the Lord?

In the dust of the streets
    lie the young and the old;
my young women and my young men
    have fallen by the sword;
you have killed them in the day of your anger,
    slaughtering without pity.

You summoned as if to a festival day
    my terrors on every side,
and on the day of the anger of the LORD
    no one escaped or survived;
those whom I held and raised
    my enemy destroyed.

פ
ע
א
ק
ר
ש

ת

*I am the man
who has seen affliction
under the rod of his wrath;*

he has driven and brought me
   into darkness without any light;
surely against me he turns his hand
   again and again the whole day long.

He has made my flesh and my skin waste away;
   he has broken my bones;
he has besieged and enveloped me
   with bitterness and tribulation;
he has made me dwell in darkness
   like the dead of long ago.

He has walled me about so that I cannot escape;
   he has made my chains heavy;
though I call and cry for help,
   he shuts out my prayer;
he has blocked my ways with blocks of stones;
   he has made my paths crooked.

He is a bear lying in wait for me,
   a lion in hiding;
he turned aside my steps and tore me to pieces;
   he has made me desolate;
he bent his bow and set me
   as a target for his arrow.

He drove into my kidneys
   the arrows of his quiver;
I have become the laughingstock of all peoples,
   the object of their taunts all day long.
He has filled me with bitterness;
   he has sated me with wormwood.

He has made my teeth grind on gravel,
   and made me cower in ashes;
my soul is bereft of peace;
   I have forgotten what good [1] is;
so I say, "My endurance has perished;
   so has my hope from the LORD."

Remember my affliction and my wanderings,
   the wormwood and the gall!
My soul continually remembers it
   and is bowed down within me.
**But this I call to mind,
   and therefore I have hope:**

**Because of the steadfast love of the LORD,
we are not cut off ,[2]**
   his mercies never come to an end;
they are new every morning;
   great is your faithfulness.

ח "The Lord is my portion," says my soul,
   "therefore I will hope in him."

The LORD is good to those who wait for him,
   to the soul who seeks him.
ט It is good that one should wait quietly
   for the salvation of the LORD.
It is good for a man that he bear
   the yoke in his youth.

י Let him sit alone in silence
   when it is laid on him;
let him put his mouth in the dust –
   there may yet be hope;
let him give his cheek to the one who strikes,
   and let him be filled with insults.

כ For the Lord will not
   cast off forever,
but, though he cause grief, he will have compassion
   according to the abundance of his steadfast love;
for he does not willingly afflict
   or grieve the children of men.

ל To crush underfoot
   all the prisoners of the earth,
to deny a man justice
   in the presence of the Most High,
to subvert a man in his lawsuit,
   the Lord does not approve.

מ Who has spoken and it came to pass,
   unless the Lord has commanded it?
Is it not from the mouth of the Most High
   that good and bad come?
Why should a living man complain,
   a man, about the punishment of his sins?

נ Let us test and examine our ways,
   and return to the LORD!
Let us lift up our hearts and hands
   to God in heaven:
We have transgressed and rebelled,
   and you have not forgiven.

ס You have wrapped yourself with anger and pursued us,
   killing without pity;
you have wrapped yourself with a cloud
   so that no prayer can pass through.
You have made us scum and garbage
   among the peoples.

All our enemies
   open their mouths against us;
panic and pitfall have come upon us,
   devastation and destruction;
my eyes flow with rivers of tears
   because of the destruction of the daughter
   of my people.

My eyes will flow without ceasing,
   without respite,
until the LORD from heaven
   looks down and sees;
my eyes cause me grief
   at the fate of all the daughters of my city.

I have been hunted like a bird
   by those who were my enemies
without cause;
they flung me alive into the pit
   and cast stones on me;
water closed over my head;
   I said, 'I am lost.'

I called on your name, O LORD,
   from the depths of the pit;
you heard my plea, 'Do not close
   your ear to my cry for help!'
You came near when I called on you;
   you said, 'Do not fear!'

You have taken up my cause, O Lord;
   you have redeemed my life.
You have seen the wrong done to me,
   O LORD, judge my cause.
You have seen all their vengeance,
   all their plots against me.

You have heard their taunts, O LORD,
   all their plots against me.
The lips and thoughts of my assailants
   are against me all the day long.
Behold their sitting and their rising;
   I am the object of their taunts.

You will repay them, O LORD,
   according to the work of their hands.
You will give them dullness of heart;
   your curse will be on them.
You will pursue them in anger
... and destroy them
   from under your heavens, O LORD.

How the gold has grown dim,
how the pure gold is changed!

The holy stones lie scattered
   at the head of every street.

The precious sons of Zion,
   worth their weight in fine gold,
how they are regarded as earthen pots,
   the work of a potter's hands!

Even jackals offer the breast;
   they nurse their young,
but the daughter of my people has become cruel,
   like the ostriches in the wilderness.

The tongue of the nursing infant sticks
   to the roof of its mouth for thirst;
the children beg for food,
   but no one gives to them.

Those who once feasted on delicacies
   perish in the streets;
those who were brought up in purple
   embrace ash heaps.

For the chastisement of the daughter of my people
 has been greater
   than the punishment of Sodom,
which was overthrown in a moment,
   and no hands were wrung for her.

Her princes were purer than snow,
   whiter than milk;
their bodies were more ruddy than coral,
   the beauty of their form was like lapis lazuli[3].

Now their face is blacker than soot;
   they are not recognized in the streets;
their skin has shriveled on their bones;
   it has become as dry as wood.

Happier were the victims of the sword
   than the victims of hunger,
who wasted away, pierced
   by lack of the fruits of the field.

The hands of compassionate women
   have boiled their own children;
they became their food
   during the destruction of the daughter of my
people.

The LORD gave full vent to his wrath;
   he poured out his hot anger,
and he kindled a fire in Zion
   that consumed its foundations.

Lamentations 4:1-11

ל **The kings of the earth did not believe,**
nor any of the inhabitants of the world,
that foe or enemy could enter
the gates of Jerusalem.

מ This was for the sins of her prophets
and the iniquities of her priests,
who shed in the midst of her
the blood of the righteous.

נ They wandered, blind, through the streets;
they were so defiled with blood
that no one was able to touch
their garments.

ס "Away! Unclean!" people cried at them.
"Away! Away! Do not touch!"
So they became fugitives and wanderers;
people said among the nations,
"They shall stay with us no longer."

פ The face of the LORD[4] has scattered them;
he will regard them no more;
no honour was shown to the priests,
no favour to the elders.

ע Our eyes failed, ever watching
vainly for help;
in our watching we watched
for a nation which could not save.

צ They dogged our steps
so that we could not walk in our streets;
our end drew near; our days were numbered,
for our end had come.

ק Our pursuers were swifter
than the eagles in the heavens;
they chased us on the mountains;
they lay in wait for us in the wilderness.

ר The breath of our nostrils, the LORD's anointed,
was captured in their pits,
of whom we said, "Under his shadow
we shall live among the nations."

ש Rejoice and be glad, O daughter of Edom,
you who dwell in the land of Uz;
but to you also the cup shall pass;
you shall become drunk and strip yourself bare.

ת **The punishment of your iniquity,**
O daughter of Zion, is accomplished;
he will keep you in exile no longer;
but your iniquity, O daughter of Edom, he will punish;
he will uncover your sins.

Remember, O Lord, what has befallen us; look, and see our disgrace!

Our inheritance has been turned over to strangers,
  our homes to foreigners.

We have become orphans, fatherless;
  our mothers are like widows.

We must pay for the water we drink;
  the wood we get must be bought.

Our pursuers are at our necks,
  we are weary; we are given no rest.

We have given the hand to Egypt, and to Assyria,
  to get bread enough.

Our fathers sinned, and are no more;
  and we bear their iniquities.

Slaves rule over us;
  there is none to deliver us from their hand.

We get our bread at the peril of our lives,
  because of the sword in the wilderness.

Our skin is hot as an oven
  with the burning heat of famine.

Women are raped in Zion,
  young women in the towns of Judah.

Princes are hung up by their hands;
  no respect is shown to the elders.

Young men are compelled to grind at the mill,
  and boys stagger under loads of wood.

The old men have left the city gate,
  the young men their music.

The joy of our hearts has ceased;
  our dancing has been turned to mourning.

The crown has fallen from our head;
  woe to us, for we have sinned!

For this our heart has become sick,
  for these things our eyes have grown dim,

for Mount Zion which lies desolate;
  jackals prowl over it.

Lamentations 5.1-18

But you, O Lord, reign forever;
   your throne endures to all generations.

Why do you forget us forever,
   why do you forsake us for so many days?

Restore us to yourself, O LORD,
that we may be restored!
   Renew our days as of old –

unless you have utterly rejected us,
   and you remain exceedingly angry with us.

Lamentations 5:19-22

Explaining this Lamentations manuscript

Changes of font in the text:

- Font changes demonstrate two voices talking across each other:
    - o   The narrator's voice is in regular font
    - o   The voice of the other survivors of Jerusalem, either personified as a widow or communal, is in *italics*

    This may be a simplification, but I wish to highlight the exchange of two viewpoints

- Imperatives are in **bold**

- Headings and emphases are in larger font size

Notes in the text:

(1) to (4) I have chosen alternative translations footnoted in the ESV.

The illustrations are of the aftermath of bushfire in the Australian Snowy Mountains

Poem 1	*Frontispiece* Snow gum, *Eucalyptus niphophila*: a desolate widow
	Borders Widow's portions
Poem 2	*Frontispiece* Snow gums consumed by fire
	Borders Charred remnants
Poem 3	*Frontispiece* Out of the ashes
	Borders summer alpine wildflowers in order of appearance, the Royal bluebell *Wahlenbergia gloriosa*, the Granite buttercup *Ranunculus graniticola*, the Grass trigger-plant, *Stylidium graminifolium*, Billy buttons *Craspedia glauca*, the Waxy bluebell *Wahlenbergia ceracea* and Common starwort *Stellaria pungens*, and the tiny new shoots of a snow gum emerging from the ground.
Poem 4	*Frontispiece* Corpse of a golden sapling
	Borders Golden remains and feather of a Nankeen Kestrel, *Falco cenchroides*, bird of prey
Poem 5	*Frontispiece* The beginnings of healing
	Borders The flowers of the Bog carraway *Oreamyrrhis ciliata* and the Alpine everlasting *Helichrysum alpinum*.

Comment

I walked in the Kosciuszko National Park in Australia's Snowy Mountains the summer after it was devastated by bushfire. It was desolate – bleached and grey, gaunt and bare – and yet austerely beautiful, its scorched leaves and regrown grass magenta and gold in the breeze. This was an appropriate visual metaphor for Lamentations: not the chaotic conflagration in blacks and reds of the siege and war for which Jerusalem's inhabitants now grieve, and from which God had not rescued them. It was written later, in the time-dragging awareness of loss, in bleak images of the aftermath of fire and demolition.

As I sketched there, I resolved on a limited palette of Australian red-gold, magenta and cyanine blue to capture the mood of the landscape, which I later used in the finished works in layer on layer of thin unmixed washes. I collected fallen remnants from the sites I sketched.

Lamentations is a set of five poems, so I designed a frontispiece for each that reflects its theme, with found objects like salvaged treasures as borders. The Hebrew letters signify the acrostic form of the first four poems, their colouring suggesting each poem's symmetry. The verse completing the acrostics (4:22) declares that God's punishment is complete. This leads to the community prayer of chapter 5.

Through the colour scheme and visual motifs, I aim to suggest the whole book's symmetry. In chapters 1 and 5, similar motifs appear, as they do in chapters 2 and 4. The last verse of chapter 5 recalls 1:1. At its centre (3:21-39) is one man's hope, based on his knowledge of God's character. His mind is crowded with unbidden images of his tragedy, but deliberately he calls to mind and restates the words by which God describes himself in Exodus 34:6, expanded in Psalm 103:8-13. It is no trite ditty drowning out the cries of anguish, no simple panacea for pain – but rather both a counterbalance and the book's pivotal point. With this in mind, I drew one of the snow gums that had been burnt to a stump within centimetres of the ground. But astonishingly, from its base new life was shooting. This is the miracle of the eucalypt: its power of resurrection after fire. All around it new plants were flowering brightly out of the charred soil, which I depict in the borders, supplementing the subdued palette with crimson and cadmium yellow.

When the community considers God in chapter 5, they are not yet so bold, seeing only their comparable status as sinners before God on his eternal throne, and aware that only God in his mercy can restore them, and they dare not presume on it. The wildflowers I depict in the paintings for this poem suggest their faith but also their tentativeness, and God's eternal nature.

Explaining this Lamentations manuscript

Ecclesiastes
Qohelet

Qohelet

Hebrew personal title rendered in Latin as Ecclesiastes, hence the English title of the book.

Probably meaning "one who gathers".

He gathers proverbs, "weighing and studying and arranging many… with great care" (Epilogue 12:9).

He gathers people to teach them knowledge (12:9).

Hebel

Hebrew, literally "vapour, mist, breath", and used throughout the text as a metaphor. Pronounced hevel.

"Various meanings glance off the surface of the word as the context shifts…" [1]

These meanings include elusive, fleeting, and insubstantial. *Hebel* is used as a metaphor for not only what it is, but what it does: it hampers vision, it shrouds in mystery.

"It is like the whole category of things it refers to: rootless, unstable, subject to continuous change… fragile, fleeting, transient." [2]

The words of Qohelet the son of David, king in Jerusalem.

**Hebel of hebel, says Qohelet,
hebel of hebel! All is hebel.**

*What does man gain by all the toil
at which he toils under the sun?*

A generation goes, and a generation comes,
but the earth remains forever.
The sun rises, and the sun goes down, and
returns panting[3] to the place where it rises.
The wind blows to the south
and goes around to the north;
around and around goes the wind,
and on its circuits the wind returns.
All streams run to the sea,
but the sea is not full;
to the place where the streams flow,
there they flow again.
All things are full of weariness;
a man cannot utter it;
the eye is not satisfied with seeing,
nor the ear filled with hearing.
What has been is what will be,
and what has been done is what will be done,
and there is nothing new under the sun.
Is there a thing of which it is said,
"See, this is new"?
It has been already
in the ages before us.
There is no remembrance of former people,
nor will there be any remembrance
of later people yet to be
among those who come after.

Qohelet have been king over Israel in Jerusalem.
And I applied my heart to seek
and to search out by wisdom
all that is done under heaven.

It is an unhappy business that God has given to the children of man to be busy with. I have seen everything that is done under the sun, and **behold**, all is *hebel* and a striving after wind.

What is crooked cannot be made straight,
and what is lacking cannot be counted.

I said in my heart, "I have acquired great wisdom, surpassing all who were over Jerusalem before me, and my heart has had great experience of wisdom and knowledge." And I applied my heart to know wisdom and to know madness and folly. I perceived that this also is but a striving after wind.

For in much wisdom is much vexation,
and he who increases knowledge increases sorrow.

I said in my heart, "Come now, I will test you with pleasure; enjoy yourself." But **behold**, this also was *hebel*.

I said of laughter, "It is mad," and of pleasure, "What use is it?" I searched with my heart how to cheer my body with wine – my heart still guiding me with wisdom – and how to lay hold on folly, till I might see what was good for the children of man to do under heaven during the few days of their life.

I made great works. I built houses and planted vineyards for myself. I made myself gardens and parks, and planted in them all kinds of fruit trees. I made myself pools from which to water the forest of growing trees. I bought male and female slaves, and had slaves who were born in my house. I had also great possessions of herds and flocks, more than any who had been before me in Jerusalem. I also gathered for myself silver and gold and the treasure of kings and provinces. I got singers, both men and women, and many concubines, the delight of the children of man. So I became great and surpassed all who were before me in Jerusalem. Also my wisdom remained with me. And whatever my eyes desired I did not keep from them. I kept my heart from no pleasure, for my heart found pleasure in all my toil, and this was my reward for all my toil.

Then I considered all that my hands had done and the toil I had expended in doing it, and **behold**, all was *hebel* and a striving after wind, and there was nothing to be gained under the sun.

So I turned to consider wisdom and madness and folly. For what can the man do who comes after the king? Only what has already been done. Then I saw that there is more *gain* in wisdom than in folly, as there is more *gain* in light than in darkness.

The wise person has his eyes in his head,
but the fool walks in darkness.

And yet I perceived that the same event happens to all of them. Then I said in my heart, "What happens to the fool will happen to me also. Why then have I been so very wise?" And I said in my heart that this also is *hebel*. For of the wise as of the fool there is no enduring remembrance, seeing that in the days to come all will have been long forgotten. How the wise dies just like the fool! So I hated life, because what is done under the sun was grievous to me, for all is *hebel* and a striving after wind.

I hated all my toil in which I toil under the sun, seeing that I must leave it to the man who will come after me, and who knows whether he will be wise or a fool? Yet he will be master of all for which I toiled and used my wisdom under the sun. This also is *hebel*.

So I turned about and gave my heart up to despair over all the toil of my labours under the sun, because sometimes a person who has toiled with wisdom and knowledge and skill must leave everything to be enjoyed by someone who did not toil for it. This also is *hebel* and a great evil.

What has a man from all the toil and striving of heart with which he toils beneath the sun? For all his days are full of sorrow, and his work is a vexation. Even in the night his heart does not rest. This also is *hebel*.

There is ***nothing better*** for a person than that he should eat and drink and find enjoyment in his toil. This also, I saw, is from the hand of God, for apart from him who can eat or who can have enjoyment? For to the one who pleases him God has given wisdom and knowledge and joy, but to the sinner he has given the business of gathering and collecting, only to give to one who pleases God. This also is *hebel* and a striving after wind.

For everything there is a season, and a time for every matter under heaven:

a time to be born, and a time to die;
a time to plant, and a time to pluck up what is planted;
a time to kill, and a time to heal;
a time to break down, and a time to build up;
a time to weep, and a time to laugh;
a time to mourn, and a time to dance;
a time to cast away stones, and a time to gather stones together;
a time to embrace, and a time to refrain from embracing;
a time to seek, and a time to lose;
a time to keep, and a time to cast away;
a time to tear, and a time to sew;
a time to keep silence, and a time to speak;
a time to love, and a time to hate;
a time for war, and a time for peace.

What gain has the worker from his toil?

I have seen the business that God has given to the children of man to be busy with. He has made everything beautiful in its time. Also, he has put eternity into man's heart, yet so that he cannot find out what God has done from the beginning to the end.

I perceived that there is *nothing better* for them than to be joyful and to do good as long as they live; also that everyone should eat and drink and take pleasure in all his toil – this is God's gift to man. I perceived that whatever God does endures forever; nothing can be added to it, nor anything taken from it. God has done it, so that people fear before him.

That which is, already has been;
that which is to be, already has been;
and God seeks what has been driven away.

Ecclesiastes 3:1-15

*Moreover, I saw under the sun
that in the place of justice,
even there was wickedness,
and in the place of righteousness,
even there was wickedness.*

I said in my heart, God will judge the righteous and the wicked, for there is a time for every matter and for every work.

I said in my heart with regard to the children of man that God is testing them that they may see that they themselves are but beasts. For what happens to the children of man and what happens to the beasts is the same; as one dies, so dies the other. They all have the same breath, and man has no **advantage** over the beasts, for all is **hebel**.

All go to one place.
All are from the dust,
and to dust all return.

Who knows whether the spirit of man goes upward and the spirit of the beast goes down into the earth?

So I saw that there is **nothing better** than that a man should rejoice in his work, for that is his lot. Who can bring him to see what will be after him?

Again I saw all the oppressions that are done under the sun. And **behold**, the tears of the oppressed, and they had no one to comfort them! On the side of their oppressors there was power, and there was no one to comfort them.

And I thought the dead who are already dead **more fortunate** than the living who are still alive. But **better** than both is he who has not yet been and has not seen the evil deeds that are done under the sun.

Then I saw that all toil and all skill in work come from a man's envy of his neighbour. This also is **hebel** and a striving after wind.

The fool folds his hands
and eats his own flesh.
Better is a handful of quietness
than two hands full of toil and a striving after wind.

Again, I saw *hebel* under the sun: one person who has no other, either son or brother, yet there is no end to all his toil, and his eyes are never satisfied with riches, so that he never asks, "For whom am I toiling and depriving myself of pleasure?" This also is *hebel* and an unhappy business.

Two are **better** than one,
because they have a good reward for their toil.
For if they fall, one will lift up his fellow.
But woe to him who is alone when he falls
and has not another to lift him up!

Again,
if two lie together, they keep warm,
but how can one keep warm alone?
And though a man might prevail against one who is alone,
two will withstand him –
a threefold cord is not quickly broken.

Better was a poor and wise youth than an old and foolish king who no longer knew how to take advice. For he went from prison to the throne, though in his own kingdom he had been born poor. I saw all the living who move about under the sun, along with that youth who was to stand in the king's place. There was no end of all the people, all of whom he led. Yet those who come later will not rejoice in him. Surely this also is *hebel* and a striving after wind.

Guard your steps when you go to the house of God.
To draw near to listen is **better** than to offer the sacrifice of fools,
for they do not know that they are doing evil.
Be not rash with your mouth,
nor let your heart be hasty to utter a word before God,
for God is in heaven and you are on earth.
Therefore let your words be few.
For a dream comes with much business,
and a fool's voice with many words.
When you vow a vow to God, do not delay paying it,
for he has no pleasure in fools.
Pay what you vow.
It is **better** that you should not vow
than that you should vow and not pay.
Let not your mouth lead you into sin,
and do not say before the messenger that it was a mistake.
Why should God be angry at your voice and destroy the work of your hands?
For when dreams increase and words grow many, there is **hebel**;
but God is the one you must fear.
If you see in a province the oppression of the poor
and the violation of justice and righteousness,
do not be amazed at the matter,
for the high official is watched by a higher,
and there are yet higher ones over them.
But this is **gain** for a land in every way:
a king committed to cultivated fields.

He who loves money will not be satisfied with money,
nor he who loves wealth with his income;
this also is *hebel*.

When goods increase, they increase who eat them, and what *advantage* has their owner but to see them with his eyes? Sweet is the sleep of a labourer, whether he eats little or much, but the full stomach of the rich will not let him sleep.

There is a grievous evil that I have seen under the sun: riches were kept by their owner to his hurt, and those riches were lost in a bad venture. And he is father of a son, but he has nothing in his hand. As he came from his mother's womb he shall go again, naked as he came, and shall take nothing for his toil that he may carry away in his hand. This also is a grievous evil: just as he came, so shall he go, and what *gain* is there to him who toils for the wind? Moreover, all his days he eats in darkness in much vexation and sickness and anger.

ehold, what I have seen to be *good and fitting* is to eat and drink and find enjoyment in all the toil with which one toils under the sun the few days of his life that God has given him, for this is his lot. Everyone also to whom God has given wealth and possessions and power to enjoy them, and to accept his lot and rejoice in his toil – this is the gift of God. For he will not much remember the days of his life because God keeps him occupied with joy in his heart.

There is an evil that I have seen under the sun, and it lies heavy on mankind: a man to whom God gives wealth, possessions, and honour, so that he lacks nothing of all that he desires, yet God does not give him power to enjoy them, but a stranger enjoys them. This is *hebel*; it is a grievous evil.

If a man fathers a hundred children and lives many years, so that the days of his years are many, but his soul is not satisfied with life's good things, and he also has no burial, I say that a stillborn child is *better off* than he. For it comes in *hebel* and goes in darkness, and in darkness its name is covered. Moreover, it has not seen the sun or known anything, yet it finds rest rather than he. Even though he should live a thousand years twice over, yet enjoy no good – do not all go to the one place? All the toil of man is for his mouth, yet his appetite is not satisfied.

For what advantage has the wise man over the fool? And what does the poor man have who knows how to conduct himself before the living?

Better is the sight of the eyes
than the wandering of the appetite:
this also is *hebel* and a striving after wind.

Whatever has come to be has already been named, and it is known what man is, and that he is not able to dispute with one stronger than he. The more words, the more *hebel*, and **what is the advantage to man?** For who knows what is good for man while he lives the few days of his *hebel* life, which he passes like a shadow? For who can tell man what will be after him under the sun?

A good name is **better** than precious ointment,
and the day of death than the day of birth.
It is **better** to go to the house of mourning
than to go to the house of feasting,
for this is the end of all mankind,
and the living will lay it to heart.
Sorrow is **better** than laughter,
for by sadness of face the heart is made glad.
The heart of the wise is in the house of mourning,
but the heart of fools is in the house of mirth.
It is **better** for a man to hear the rebuke of the wise
than to hear the song of fools.
For as the crackling of thorns under a pot,
so is the laughter of the fools;
this also is *hebel*.

Surely oppression drives the wise into madness,
and a bribe corrupts the heart.
Better is the end of a thing than its beginning,
and the patient in spirit is **better** than the proud in spirit.
Be not quick in your spirit to become angry,
for anger lodges in the bosom of fools.
Say not, "Why were the former days better than these?"
For it is not from wisdom that you ask this.
Wisdom is **good** with an inheritance,
an **advantage** to those who see the sun.
For the protection of wisdom is like the protection of money,
and the **advantage** of knowledge
is that wisdom preserves the life of him who has it.
Consider the work of God:
who can make straight what he has made crooked?
In the day of prosperity be joyful,
and in the day of adversity consider:
God has made the one as well as the other,
so that man may not find out anything that will be after him.

In my *hebel* life I have seen everything. There is a righteous man who perishes in his righteousness, and there is a wicked man who prolongs his life in his evildoing.

Be not overly righteous, and do not make yourself too wise.
Why should you destroy yourself?
Be not overly wicked, neither be a fool.
Why should you die before your time?
It is **good** that *you should take hold of this,*
and from that withhold not your hand,
for the one who fears God shall come out from both of them.
Wisdom gives strength to the wise man
more than ten rulers who are in a city.
Surely there is not a righteous man on earth who does good and never sins.
Do not take to heart all the things that people say,
lest you hear your servant cursing you.
Your heart knows that many times
you have yourself cursed others.

All this I have tested by wisdom. I said, "I will be wise," but it was far from me. That which has been is far off, and deep, very deep; who can find it out?

I turned my heart to know and to search out and to seek wisdom and the scheme of things, and to know the wickedness of folly and the foolishness that is madness. And I find something more bitter than death: the woman whose heart is snares and nets, and whose hands are fetters. He who pleases God escapes her, but the sinner is taken by her.

Behold, this is what I found, says Qohelet, while adding one thing to another to find the scheme of things – which my soul has sought repeatedly, but I have not found. One man among a thousand I found, but a woman among all these I have not found. See, this alone I found, that God made man upright, but they have sought out many schemes.

Who is like the wise?
And who knows the interpretation
of a thing?

A man's wisdom makes his face shine,
and the hardness of his face is changed.
I say:
Keep the king's command, because of God's oath to him.
Be not hasty to go from his presence.
Do not take your stand in an evil cause, for he does whatever he pleases.
For the word of the king is supreme,
and who may say to him, "What are you doing?"
Whoever keeps a command will know no evil thing,
and the wise heart will know the proper time and the just way.
For there is a time and a way for everything,
although man's trouble lies heavy on him.
For he does not know what is to be,
for who can tell him how it will be?
No man has power to retain the spirit,
or power over the day of death.
There is no discharge from war,
nor will wickedness deliver those who are given to it.

All this I observed while applying my heart to all that is done under the sun, when man had power over man to his hurt. Then I saw the wicked buried. They used to go in and out of the holy place and were praised in the city where they had done such things. This also is *hebel*.

Because the sentence against an evil deed is not executed speedily, the heart of the children of man is fully set to do evil. Though a sinner does evil a hundred times and prolongs his life, yet I know that it will be well with those who fear God, because they fear before him. But it will not be well with the wicked, neither will he prolong his days like a shadow, because he does not fear before God.

There is a *hebel* that takes place on earth, that there are righteous people to whom it happens according to the deeds of the wicked, and there are wicked people to whom it happens according to the deeds of the righteous. I said that this also is *hebel*.

And I commend joy, for man has **no good thing under the sun but** to eat and drink and be joyful, for this will go with him in his toil through the days of his life that God has given him under the sun.

When I applied my heart to know wisdom, and to see the business that is done on earth, how neither day nor night do one's eyes see sleep, then I saw all the work of God, that man cannot find out the work that is done under the sun. However much man may toil in seeking, he will not find it out. Even though a wise man claims to know, he cannot find it out.

But all this I laid to heart, examining it all, how the righteous and the wise and their deeds are in the hand of God. Whether it is love or hate, man does not know; both are before him.

It is the same for all, since the same event happens to the righteous and the wicked, to the good and the evil, to the clean and the unclean, to him who sacrifices and him who does not sacrifice. As is the good, so is the sinner, and he who swears is as he who shuns an oath. This is an evil in all that is done under the sun, that the same event happens to all. Also, the hearts of the children of man are full of evil, and madness is in their hearts while they live, and after that they go to the dead. But he who is joined with all the living has hope, for a living dog is better than a dead lion. For the living know that they will die, but the dead know nothing, and they have no more reward, for the memory of them is forgotten. Their love and their hate and their envy have already perished, and forever they have no more share in all that is done under the sun.

Go, eat your bread in joy,
and drink your wine with a merry heart,
for God has already approved what you do.
Let your garments be always white
Let not oil be lacking on your head.
Enjoy life with the wife whom you love,
*all the days of your **hebel** life*
that he has given you under the sun,
because that is your portion in life
and in your toil at which you toil under the sun.
Whatever your hand finds to do,
do it with your might,
for there is no work or thought or knowledge or wisdom in Sheol,
to which you are going.

Again I saw that under the sun the race is not to the swift, nor the battle to the strong, nor bread to the wise, nor riches to the intelligent, nor favour to those with knowledge, but time and chance happen to them all. For man does not know his time. Like fish that are taken in an evil net, and like birds that are caught in a snare, so the children of man are snared at an evil time, when it suddenly falls upon them.

I have also seen this example of wisdom under the sun, and it seemed great to me. There was a little city with few men in it, and a great king came against it and besieged it, building great siegeworks against it. But there was found in it a poor, wise man, and he by his wisdom delivered the city. Yet no one remembered that poor man. But I say that

wisdom is **better** than might,
though the poor man's wisdom is despised and his words are not heard.
The words of the wise heard in quiet
are **better** than the shouting of a ruler among fools.
Wisdom is **better** than weapons of war,
but one sinner destroys much good.
Dead flies make the perfumer's ointment give off a stench;
so a little folly outweighs wisdom and honour.
A wise man's heart inclines him to the right,
but a fool's heart to the left.
Even when the fool walks on the road, he lacks sense,
and he says to everyone that he is a fool.
If the anger of the ruler rises against you, do not leave your place,
for calmness will lay great offenses to rest.

There is an evil that I have seen under the sun, as it were an error proceeding from the ruler: folly is set in many high places, and the rich sit in a low place. I have seen slaves on horses, and princes walking on the ground like slaves.

He who digs a pit will fall into it,
and a serpent will bite him who breaks through a wall.
He who quarries stones is hurt by them,
and he who splits logs is endangered by them.

If the iron is blunt, and one does not sharpen the edge,
he must use more strength,
but wisdom is *an advantage to success.*[4]
If the serpent bites before it is charmed,
there is no *advantage* to the charmer.

The words of a wise man's mouth win him *favour,*
but the lips of a fool consume him.
The beginning of the words of his mouth is foolishness,
and the end of his talk is evil madness.

A fool multiplies words,
though no man knows what is to be,
and who can tell him what will be after him?
The toil of a fool wearies him,
for he does not know the way to the city.

Woe to you, O land, when your king is a child,
and your princes feast in the morning!
Happy are you, O land, when your king is the son of the nobility,
and your princes feast at the proper time,
for strength, and not for drunkenness!

Through sloth the roof sinks in,
and through indolence the house leaks.
Bread is made for laughter,
and wine gladdens life,
and money answers everything.

Even in your thought, do not curse the king,
nor in your bedroom curse the rich,
for a bird of the air will carry your voice,
or some winged creature tell the matter.

Cast your bread upon the waters for you will find it after many days.

Give a portion to seven, or even to eight,
for you know not what disaster may happen on earth.

If the clouds are full of rain, they empty themselves on the earth,
and if a tree falls to the south or to the north,
in the place where the tree falls, there it will lie.

He who observes the wind will not sow,
and he who regards the clouds will not reap.

As you do not know the way of the wind,
or how the bones grow in the womb of a woman with child, [(5)]
so you do not know the work of God who makes everything.

In the morning sow your seed, and at evening withhold not your hand,
for you do not know which will prosper, this or that,
or whether both alike will be good.

Light is sweet, and it is pleasant for the eyes to see the sun.
So if a person lives many years,
let him rejoice in them all;
but let him remember *that the days of darkness will be many.*
All that comes is **hebel**.

Rejoice, O young man, in your youth,
and let your heart cheer you in the days of your youth.
Walk in the ways of your heart and the sight of your eyes.
But know that for all these things
God will bring you into judgment.
Remove vexation from your heart,
and put away evil [(6)] *from your body,*
for youth and the dawn of life are **hebel**.

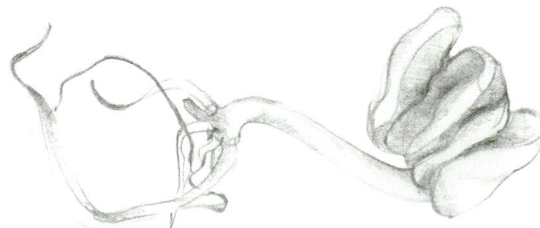

Remember also your Creator in the days of your youth,
before the evil days come and the years draw near
of which you will say "I have no pleasure in them";
before the sun and the light and the moon and the stars are darkened
and the clouds return after the rain,
in the day when the keepers of the house tremble,
and the strong men are bent,
and the grinders cease because they are few,
and those who look through the windows are dimmed,
and the doors on the street are shut –
when the sound of the grinding is low,
and one rises up at the sound of a bird,
and all the daughters of song are brought low –
they are afraid also of what is high,
and terrors are in the way;
the almond tree blossoms,
the grasshopper drags itself along,
and desire fails,
because man is going to his eternal home,
and the mourners go about the streets –
before the silver cord is snapped,
or the golden bowl is broken,
or the pitcher is shattered at the fountain,
or the wheel broken at the cistern,
and the dust returns to the earth as it was,
and the spirit returns to God who gave it.

Hebel of hebel, says Qohelet; all is hebel.

Besides being wise,
Qohelet also taught the people knowledge,
weighing and studying and arranging many proverbs with great care.
Qohelet sought to find words of delight,
and uprightly he wrote words of truth.
The words of the wise are like goads,
and like nails firmly fixed are the collected sayings;
they are given by one Shepherd.

My son, beware of anything beyond these.
Of making many books there is no end,
and much study is a weariness of the flesh.

The end of the matter; all has been heard.

Fear God and keep his commandments,
for this is the whole of man.[7]
For God will bring every deed into judgment,
with every secret thing, whether good or evil.

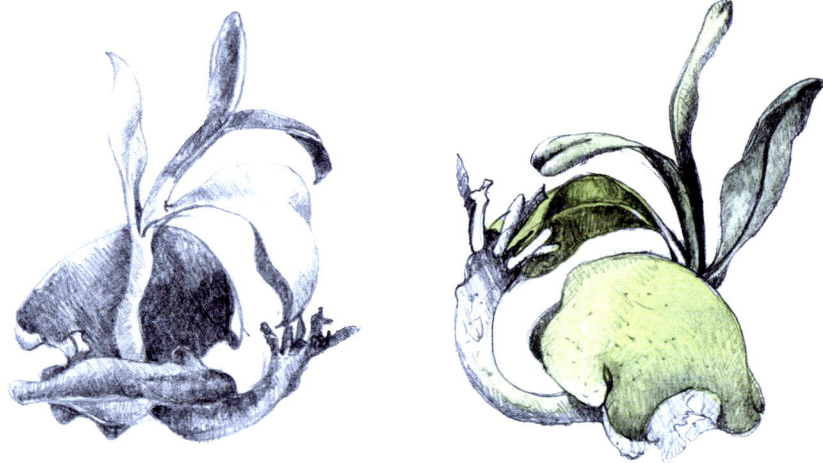

Explaining this Ecclesiastes manuscript

Changes of font in the text

- Headings are in larger font size

- Emphases are in **bold**, including **behold**, code word for "pay attention"

- Major headings are **large and bold**

- Key issues are in ***bold italics***:
    - Qohelet's quest

    - His conclusions in two main categories:
        - What is of no gain: foolish and ***hebel***
        - What is of gain or advantage: ***better*** and ***the best***

- Imperatives are in *italics*

Notes in the text

(1) Eugene H Peterson 1992
Five Smooth Stones for Pastoral Work page 153
Grand Rapids: Eerdmans.

(2) Barry G Webb 2000
Five Festal Garments: Christian Reflections on the Song of Songs, Ruth, Lamentations, Ecclesiastes and Esther
pages 90, 100
Leicester: Inter-Varsity Press.

(3) and (4) In order to connect words to wider themes in the book, I have chosen alternatives footnoted in the ESV.

(5) Alternatively, this is translated in the ESV *the way the spirit comes to the bones in the womb of a mother with child*, connecting this passage to *spirit* in 3:12 and 12:7.

(6) I use the translation used in the ESV footnote *evil*, thus repeating a word used elsewhere in the text, to link it with the major theme of what is good and what is not. It is not implying a moral judgement.

(7) I have amended the ESV text of 12:13b to remove the word *duty* that is not in the original Hebrew. The whole person is grounded and finds meaning in this obedience. Life is not a duty, but a response. Gift, not task, is the essence of life.

Title Page	The bay at pre-dawn
Pages 60-61	*Left* Pre-dawn mist
	Right Roots of the Grey mangrove, *Avicennia marina*: "whose words are like goads"
Pages 62-63	*Left* Light blue soldier crab, *Mictyris longicarpus*, and juvenile
	Right Soldier crab dwellings and the incoming tide: the *hebel* of achievement
Pages 64-65	*Left* Cruciform symmetry of the seemingly scruffy mangrove: "God seeks what has been driven away"
	Right Clear day dawning: the big picture under heaven
Pages 66-67	*Left* Tideline: "to dust all return"
	Right Migratory Whimbrels, *Numenius phaeopus*: "two are better than one"
Pages 68-69	*Left* Stormy sky: "God is in heaven"
	Mangrove in fruit
	Right Mangrove leaf blowing in the wind
Pages 70-71	*Left* Oysters (*Saccostrea glomerate*) on a rock: "Who can make straight what God has made crooked?"
	Right Mangrove at high tide: deep and far off
Pages 72-73	*Left* Oyster remains on driftwood: burial site
	Right Hercules' club whelk, *Pyrazus ebeninus*: from life on the mudflats to Sheol
Pages 74-75	*Left* Turtle skull washed up: "like fish in a snare"
	The trail of a Dark-mouthed Conniwink, *Bembicium melanostoma* and footprints of a bird: the aimless and the direct
	Right Patterns in the sand of tidal ridges and stingrays' resting places: "he who digs a pit will fall into it"
Pages 76-77	*Left* Fine day rejoicing; mangrove seeds awaiting the tide: "cast your bread on the waters... it is pleasant for the eyes to see the sun"
	Right Mangrove seeds germinating: "in the morning sow your seed"
Pages 78-79	*Left* Mangrove seeds in shallow water: *hebel* and sun, air and water, life and death, goads and nails
	Right Mangrove seedlings: sowing prospers

As the character Qohelet ponders the ebb and flow of life and death, the cycles of nature and the patterns of human behaviour, he seeks to discern what is of lasting value from that which is *hebel* (fleeting and insubstantial), and what is wise from that which is foolish. He talks of sun and cloud, mist and wind, seeds and society.

As I explored the mudflats at Tahlee on the shores of Port Stephens on the mid NSW coast, I saw the mangroves dropping their seeds into the high tide, to be washed to new resting places to take root and grow. What an image for 11:1! I realised then how appropriate this setting was for Ecclesiastes: the ebb and flow of the tides; the life that thrives on their cycle – shellfish and mangroves, wading birds and crabs; the debris abandoned on the tide-line; the early morning mist and the seaweed caught around the mangroves fluttering in the wind; the panoramic view of the bay.

The mangroves, scruffy at first glance, revealed an ordered symmetry on closer inspection. It reminded me of the curator's comment next to Pissarro's painting, *La Place du Theatre Français 1898* at an exhibition at the Art Gallery of NSW in 2006, "Its informality is deceptive; it is a vigorously ordered and integrated universe he shows us here, with not one speck redundant or out of place." It applies equally to the form of Ecclesiastes that 12:9 tells us was arranged with great care.

I painted the landscape in cloud and mist, sunshine and wind, predawn and daylight. From this dual focus on text and landscape evolved this manuscript, after many rearrangements of its format. I offer it as one of many ways of seeing such a kaleidoscopic work. I should subtitle it "where angels fear to tread".

I suggest Qohelet's journey by the predawn of the first paintings to the full daylight of the last, and his understanding by the mangrove flower's development to seed and its germination.

The long middle section beginning "Moreover I saw under the sun" (3:16–10:20), I divide into two groups of cameos that Qohelet empirically observes and to which he offers a pragmatic "better" solution, interspersed with instructions and "the best". I think some of these units are symmetrical, for example 5:10–6:9, and the last poem (10:8-20), whose first verse parallels the last, thus "he who digs a pit" equates with sedition. The first group (3:16–7:24) looks at life and society in general, and the second (8:1–10:20) responsibilities of leadership in particular. In the centre of each group is "the best" way of responding to life, which I highlight by decorative initial letter. Between them is a restatement of Qohelet's quest and response (7:25-29). It is as though he has looked down and around him, just as I have drawn subjects on and about the mudflats to separate these cameos. I call this whole section "life under the sun".

Flanked on either side of this long section are two shorter ones (3:1-15 and 11:1-10), which I accompany with two landscapes which, slightly overlapping, form one panoramic view of the bay as I look up from the mudflats, and into which all the cameo drawings find their place. That is how I respond to these passages. The first I see as "the big picture": this is what life looks like between Eden and eternity, and how we ought to respond. It is seen under heaven, where God dwells (5:1), and without *hebel*. Read Genesis 1-3, in which God's good world is marred (though not destroyed) by evil. See how many of its ideas are embedded here – and scattered throughout the book.

The second passage advises how to live in this world from this perspective: not waiting on the edge, but immersed in it – risk-takingly, generously and thankfully engaged in it. I have divided it into two symmetrical stanzas. In the first, the first and last verses are in parallel: cast your bread/ sow your seed. In the central verse: don't hold back from life by indecision. In the second stanza, while the sun is still pleasant, and life past and future is *hebel*, rejoice.

The first landscape is of the beauty of a cloudless dawn. The second is of a fine day whose wispy *hebel* may dissipate in the wind, or join forces to form rain-clouds. The little tree is sowing seeds to be cast into the waters. It is this perspective of the panorama under heaven that enables Qohelet to offer the "best" advice throughout the book. Look at his report: the way he shifts from past to present tense, and from observation to consideration, conclusion and imperative voice.

Prefacing his big picture is Qohelet's "autobiography" – his quest sought "under heaven" but carried out "under the sun" – what he achieved and how he measured it (1:12–2:11), and later, after much consideration, what he concluded (2:12-26). I draw soldier crabs and their dwellings under the imminent flooding of the tide to suggest the transience of achievement.

Like mounts around this big view of the world and Qohelet's grand quest are two poems that place it in context. The first is of the cycles of the natural world (1:4-11); the second of the last cycle of human (perhaps Qohelet's) life (12:1-7).

Surrounding the whole work is a double frame: the inner, negative assessment of *hebel* (1:3 and 12:8), and the outer, positive and objective assessment of Qohelet's words as wise goads (1:1 and 12:9-14). Thus, my drawings of mangrove roots separate the Prologue and Epilogue (the outer frame) from the remainder of the book.

By organising the text this way I seek to suggest that the writer is presenting two worldviews: the materialistic (reality exists only in what can be apprehended through human senses), which yields pragmatic (albeit good) advice. The other encompasses and extends the first from a wider perspective of faith in God in heaven, who is described through his scriptures, to which the writer subtly alludes. Only when he has addressed this issue of worldview, can the writer let it fade into the background, and shift our focus to the overriding quest: what *is* of gain? (1:3 and repeated throughout). I suggest you read the whole and list what is of gain and what is not. Each has two categories: on the one hand, better and the best (including instructions in italics); and on the other, *hebel* or worse, foolish.

I think Ecclesiastes is about contentment. The writer is presenting a choice between seeing life as a gift to be enjoyed with others and with thanks (which brings gain); or as tasks to be achieved (which is *hebel*). For how we use that gift, we are accountable to God.

In the paintings, I have used both the colour palettes of Lamentations and Ruth – the bleak and the pure – though I have substituted Australian red gold with gold ochre, whose earthiness gives a soft grainy effect for cloud and sand. This palette expresses both the positive and negative tenors of the book. The illustrations are unadorned; some even are the field sketches I made as I balanced in the mud. I wanted a spare, pared-back realism. I wanted to convey the book's seemingly piecemeal form, its subtlety, its combination of first impressions and considered conclusions, its balance of what is or is not *hebel*, life and death, and negative and positive tenors.

If I began the exercise again, would I do it differently – a different habitat, a different layout? Quite possibly... After all, its structure is *hebel*, including the divisions between prose and poetry and proverb – just like its character Qohelet. Try it for yourself: take a copy of the text, remove divisions and references, and format it into one long piece of prose – and consider and debate your ideas in a group of fellow seekers. Then, when you know what your questions are, see how the experts have answered them.

Esther

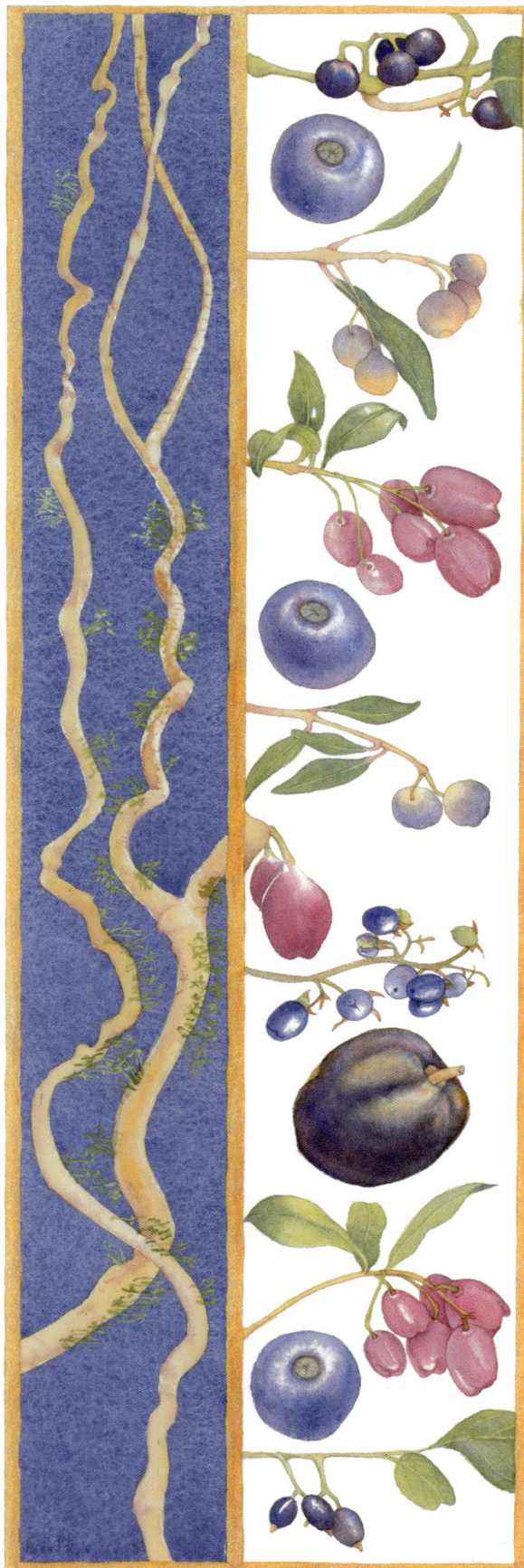

Now

*in the days of Ahasuerus,
the Ahasuerus who reigned
from India to Ethiopia
over 127 provinces,*

in those days when King Ahasuerus sat on his royal throne in Susa, the capital, in the third year of his reign he gave a feast for all his officials and servants. The army of Persia and Media and the nobles and governors of the provinces were before him, while he showed the riches of his royal glory and the splendour and pomp of his greatness for many days, 180 days.

And when these days were completed, the king gave for all the people present in Susa, the citadel, both great and small, a feast lasting for seven days in the court of the garden of the king's palace. There were white cotton curtains and violet hangings fastened with cords of fine linen and purple to silver rods and marble pillars, and also couches of gold and silver on a mosaic pavement of porphyry, marble, mother-of-pearl and precious stones. Drinks were served in golden vessels, vessels of different kinds, and the royal wine was lavished according to the bounty of the king. And drinking was according to this edict: "There is no compulsion." For the king had given orders to all the staff of his palace to do as each man desired.

Queen Vashti also gave a feast for the women in the palace that belonged to King Ahasuerus.

On the seventh day,

when the heart of the king was merry with wine, he commanded Mehuman, Biztha, Harbona, Bigtha and Abagtha, Zethar and Carkas, the seven eunuchs who served in the presence of King Ahasuerus, to bring Queen Vashti before the king with her royal crown, in order to show the peoples and the princes her beauty, for she was lovely to look at. But Queen Vashti refused to come at the king's command delivered by the eunuchs. At this the king became enraged, and his anger burned within him.

Then the king said to the wise men who knew the times (for this was the king's procedure toward all who were versed in law and judgment, the men next to him being Carshena, Shethar, Admatha, Tarshish, Meres, Marsena, and Memucan, the seven princes of Persia and Media, who saw the king's face, and sat first in the kingdom): "According to the law, what is to be done to Queen Vashti, because she has not performed the command of King Ahasuerus delivered by the eunuchs?"

Then Memucan said in the presence of the king and the officials, "Not only against the king has Queen Vashti done wrong, but also against all the officials and all the peoples who are in all the provinces of King Ahasuerus. For the queen's behaviour will be made known to all women, causing them to look at their husbands with contempt, since they will say, 'King Ahasuerus commanded Queen Vashti to be brought before him, and she did not come.' This very day the noble women of Persia and Media who have heard of the queen's behaviour will say the same to all the king's officials, and there will be contempt and wrath in plenty. If it please the king, let a royal order go out from him, and let it be written among the laws of the Persians and the Medes so that it may not be repealed, that Vashti is never again to come before King Ahasuerus. And let the king give her royal position to another who is better than she. So when the decree made by the king is proclaimed throughout all his kingdom, for it is vast, all women will give honour to their husbands, high and low alike."

This advice pleased the king and the princes, and the king did as Memucan proposed. He sent letters to all the royal provinces, to every province in its own script and to every people in its own language, *that every man be master in his own household and speak according to the language of his people.*

After these things,

when the anger of King Ahasuerus had abated, he remembered Vashti and what she had done and what had been decreed against her. Then the king's young men who attended him said, "Let beautiful young virgins be sought out for the king. And let the king appoint officers in all the provinces of his kingdom to gather all the beautiful young virgins to the harem in Susa the capital, under custody of Hegai, the king's eunuch, who is in charge of the women. Let their cosmetics be given them. And let the young woman who pleases the king be queen instead of Vashti." This pleased the king, and he did so.

Now there was a Jew in Susa the citadel whose name was Mordecai, the son of Jair, son of Shimei, son of Kish, a Benjaminite, who had been carried away from Jerusalem among the captives carried away with Jeconiah king of Judah, whom Nebuchadnezzar king of Babylon had carried away. He was bringing up Hadassah, that is Esther, the daughter of his uncle, for she had neither father nor mother. The young woman had a beautiful figure and was lovely to look at, and when her father and her mother died, Mordecai took her as his own daughter. So when the king's order and his edict were proclaimed, and when many young women were gathered in Susa the citadel in custody of Hegai, Esther also was taken into the king's palace and put in custody of Hegai, who had charge of the women. And the young woman pleased him and won his favour. And he quickly provided her with her cosmetics and her portion of food, and with seven chosen young women from the king's palace, and advanced her and her young women to the best place in the harem. Esther had not made known her people or kindred, for Mordecai had commanded her not to make it known. And every day Mordecai walked in front of the court of the harem to learn how Esther was and what was happening to her.

Now when the turn came for each young woman to go in to King Ahasuerus, after being twelve months under the regulations for the women, since this was the regular period of their beautifying, six months with oil of myrrh and six months with spices and ointments for women – when the young woman went in to the king in this way, she was given whatever she desired to take with her from the harem to the king's palace. In the evening she would go in, and in the morning she would return to the second harem in custody of Shaashgaz, the king's eunuch, who was in charge of the concubines. She would not go in to the king again, unless the king delighted in her and she was summoned by name.

When the turn came for Esther the daughter of Abihail the uncle of Mordecai, who had taken her as his own daughter, to go in to the king, she asked for nothing except what Hegai the king's eunuch, who had charge of the women, advised.

Now Esther was winning favour in the eyes of all who saw her.

And when Esther was taken to King Ahasuerus into his royal palace *in the tenth month, which is the month of Tebeth, in the seventh year of his reign,* the king loved Esther more than all the women, and she won grace and favour in his sight more than all the virgins, so that he set the royal crown on her head and made her queen instead of Vashti.

Then the king gave a great feast for all his officials and servants; it was Esther's feast. He also granted a remission of taxes to the provinces and gave gifts with royal generosity.

$\mathcal{N}$ow

when the virgins were gathered together the second time,

Mordecai was sitting at the king's gate. Esther had not made known her kindred or her people, as Mordecai had commanded her, for Esther obeyed Mordecai just as when she was brought up by him.

In those days, as Mordecai was sitting at the king's gate, Bigthan and Teresh, two of the king's eunuchs, who guarded the threshold, became angry and sought to lay hands on King Ahasuerus. And this came to the knowledge of Mordecai, and he told it to Queen Esther, and Esther told the king in the name of Mordecai. When the affair was investigated and found to be so, the men were both hanged on the gallows. And it was recorded in the book of the chronicles in the presence of the king.

After these things,

King Ahasuerus promoted Haman the Agagite, the son of Hammedatha, and advanced him and set his throne above all the officials who were with him. And all the king's servants who were at the king's gate bowed down and paid homage to Haman, for the king had so commanded concerning him. But Mordecai did not bow down or pay homage. Then the king's servants who were at the king's gate said to Mordecai, "Why do you transgress the king's command?" And when they spoke to him day after day and he would not listen to them, they told Haman, in order to see whether Mordecai's words would stand, for he had told them that he was a Jew. And when Haman saw that Mordecai did not bow down or pay homage to him, Haman was filled with fury. But he disdained to lay hands on Mordecai alone. So, as they had made known to him the people of Mordecai, Haman sought to destroy all the Jews, the people of Mordecai, throughout the whole kingdom of Ahasuerus.

In the first month, which is the month of Nisan, in the twelfth year of King Ahasuerus, they cast Pur

(that is, they cast lots) before Haman day after day; and they cast it month after month till the twelfth month, which is the month of Adar. Then Haman said to King Ahasuerus, "There is a certain people scattered abroad and dispersed among the peoples in all the provinces of your kingdom. Their laws are different from those of every other people, and they do not keep the king's laws, so that it is not to the king's profit to tolerate them. If it please the king, let it be decreed that they be destroyed, and I will pay 10,000 talents[1] of silver into the hands of those who have charge of the king's business, that they may put it into the king's treasuries." So the king took his signet ring from his hand and gave it to Haman the Agagite, the son of Hammedatha, the enemy of the Jews. And the king said to Haman, "The money is given to you, the people also, to do with them as it seems good to you."

Then the king's scribes were summoned on the thirteenth day of the first month, and an edict, according to all that Haman commanded, was written to the king's satraps and to the governors over all the provinces and to the officials of all the peoples, to every province in its own script and every people in its own language. It was written in the name of King Ahasuerus and sealed with the king's signet ring. Letters were sent by couriers to all the king's provinces with instruction *to destroy, to kill, and to annihilate all Jews, young and old, women and children, in one day, the thirteenth day of the twelfth month, which is the month of Adar, and to plunder their goods.* A copy of the document was to be issued as a decree in every province by proclamation to all the peoples to be ready for that day. The couriers went out hurriedly by order of the king, and the decree was issued in Susa the citadel.

And the king and Haman sat down to drink, but the city of Susa was thrown into confusion.

When

Mordecai learned all that had been done,

Mordecai tore his clothes and put on sackcloth and ashes, and went out into the midst of the city, and he cried out with a loud and bitter cry. He went up to the entrance of the king's gate, for no one was allowed to enter the king's gate clothed in sackcloth. And in every province, wherever the king's command and his decree reached, there was great mourning among the Jews, with fasting and weeping and lamenting, and many of them lay in sackcloth and ashes.

When Esther's young women and her eunuchs came and told her, the queen was deeply distressed. She sent garments to clothe Mordecai, so that he might take off his sackcloth, but he would not accept them. Then Esther called for Hathach, one of the king's eunuchs, who had been appointed to attend her, and ordered him to go to Mordecai to learn what this was and why it was. Hathach went out to Mordecai in the open square of the city in front of the king's gate, and Mordecai told him all that had happened to him, and the exact sum of money that Haman had promised to pay into the king's treasuries for the destruction of the Jews. Mordecai also gave him a copy of the written decree issued in Susa for their destruction, that he might show it to Esther and explain it to her and command her to go to the king to beg his favour and plead with him on behalf of her people. And Hathach went and told Esther what Mordecai had said.

Then Esther spoke to Hathach and commanded him to go to Mordecai and say, "All the king's servants and the people of the king's provinces know that if any man or woman goes to the king inside the inner court without being called, there is but one law – to be put to death, except the one to whom the king holds out the golden scepter so that he may live. But as for me, I have not been called to come in to the king these thirty days." And they told Mordecai what Esther had said.

Then Mordecai told them to reply to Esther,

Do not think to yourself that in the king's palace you will escape any more than all the other Jews. For if you keep silent at this time, relief and deliverance will rise for the Jews from another place, but you and your father's house will perish. And who knows whether you have not come to the kingdom for such a time as this?"

Then Esther told them to reply to Mordecai,

"Go, gather all the Jews to be found in Susa, and hold a fast on my behalf, and do not eat or drink for three days, night or day. I and my young women will also fast as you do. Then I will go to the king, though it is against the law, and if I perish, I perish."

Mordecai then went away and did everything as Esther had ordered him.

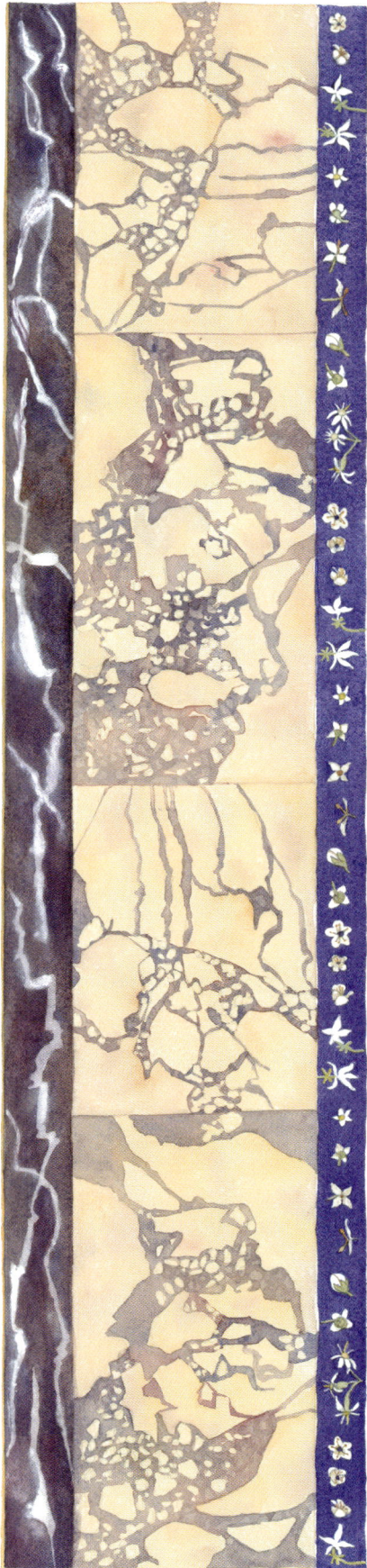

On the third day Esther put on her royal robes

and stood in the inner court of the king's palace, in front of the king's quarters, while the king was sitting on his royal throne inside the throne room opposite the entrance to the palace. And when the king saw Queen Esther standing in the court, she won favor in his sight, and he held out to Esther the golden scepter that was in his hand. Then Esther approached and touched the tip of the scepter. And the king said to her, "What is it, Queen Esther? What is your request? It shall be given you, even to the half of my kingdom."

And Esther said, "If it please the king, let the king and Haman come today to a feast that I have prepared for the king." Then the king said, "Bring Haman quickly, so that we may do as Esther has asked." So the king and Haman came to the feast that Esther had prepared.

And as they were drinking wine after the feast, the king said to Esther, "What is your wish? It shall be granted you. And what is your request? Even to the half of my kingdom, it shall be fulfilled." Then Esther answered, "My wish and my request is: If I have found favour in the sight of the king, and if it please the king to grant my wish and fulfil my request, let the king and Haman come to the feast that I will prepare for them, and tomorrow I will do as the king has said."

And Haman went out that day joyful and glad of heart.

But when Haman saw Mordecai in the king's gate, that he neither rose nor trembled before him, he was filled with wrath against Mordecai. Nevertheless, Haman restrained himself and went home, and he sent and brought his friends and his wife Zeresh.

And Haman recounted to them the splendour of his riches, the number of his sons, all the promotions with which the king had honoured him, and how he had advanced him above the officials and the servants of the king. Then Haman said, "Even Queen Esther let no one but me come with the king to the feast she prepared. And tomorrow also I am invited by her together with the king. Yet all this is worth nothing to me, so long as I see Mordecai the Jew sitting at the king's gate."

Then his wife Zeresh and all his friends said to him, "Let a gallows fifty cubits[2] high be made, and in the morning tell the king to have Mordecai hanged upon it. Then go joyfully with the king to the feast." This idea pleased Haman, and he had the gallows made.

On
that night
the king could not sleep.

And he gave orders to bring the book of memorable deeds, the chronicles, and they were read before the king. And it was found written how Mordecai had told about Bigthana and Teresh, two of the king's eunuchs, who guarded the threshold, and who had sought to lay hands on King Ahasuerus. And the king said, "What honour or distinction has been bestowed on Mordecai for this?" The king's young men who attended him said, "Nothing has been done for him."

And the king said, "Who is in the court?" Now Haman had just entered the outer court of the king's palace to speak to the king about having Mordecai hanged on the gallows that he had prepared for him. And the king's young men told him, "Haman is there, standing in the court." And the king said, "Let him come in." So Haman came in, and the king said to him, "What should be done to the man whom the king delights to honour?" And Haman said to himself, "Whom would the king delight to honour more than me?" And Haman said to the king, "For the man whom the king delights to honour, let royal robes be brought, which the king has worn, and the horse that the king has ridden, and on whose head a royal crown is set. And let the robes and the horse be handed over to one of the king's most noble officials. Let them dress the man whom the king delights to honour, and let them lead him on the horse through the square of the city, proclaiming before him: 'Thus shall it be done to the man whom the king delights to honour.'" Then the king said to Haman, "Hurry; take the robes and the horse, as you have said, and do so to Mordecai the Jew who sits at the king's gate. Leave out nothing that you have mentioned."

So Haman took the robes and the horse, and he dressed Mordecai and led him through the square of the city, proclaiming before him, "Thus shall it be done to the man whom the king delights to honour."

Then

Mordecai returned to the king's gate. But Haman hurried to his house, mourning and with his head covered.

And Haman told his wife Zeresh and all his friends everything that had happened to him. Then his wise men and his wife Zeresh said to him, "If Mordecai, before whom you have begun to fall, is of the Jewish people, you will not overcome him but will surely fall before him."

While they were yet talking with him, the king's eunuchs arrived and hurried to bring Haman to the feast that Esther had prepared.

So the king and Haman went in to feast with Queen Esther.

And on the second day, as they were drinking wine after the feast, the king again said to Esther, "What is your wish, Queen Esther? It shall be granted you. And what is your request? Even to the half of my kingdom, it shall be fulfilled."

Then Queen Esther answered, "If I have found favor in your sight, O king, and if it please the king, let my life be granted me for my wish, and my people for my request. For we have been sold, I and my people, to be destroyed, to be killed, and to be annihilated. If we had been sold merely as slaves, men and women, I would have been silent, for our affliction is not to be compared with the loss to the king."

Then King Ahasuerus said to Queen Esther, "Who is he, and where is he, who has dared to do this?" And Esther said, "A foe and enemy! This wicked Haman!" Then Haman was terrified before the king and the queen.

And the king arose in his wrath from the wine-drinking and went into the palace garden, but Haman stayed to beg for his life from Queen Esther, for he saw that harm was determined against him by the king. And the king returned from the palace garden to the place where they were drinking wine, as Haman was falling on the couch where Esther was. And the king said, "Will he even assault the queen in my presence, in my own house?" As the word left the mouth of the king, they covered Haman's face.

Then Harbona, one of the eunuchs in attendance on the king, said, "Moreover, the gallows that Haman has prepared for Mordecai, whose word saved the king, is standing at Haman's house, fifty cubits high." And the king said, "Hang him on that." So they hanged Haman on the gallows that he had prepared for Mordecai. Then the wrath of the king abated.

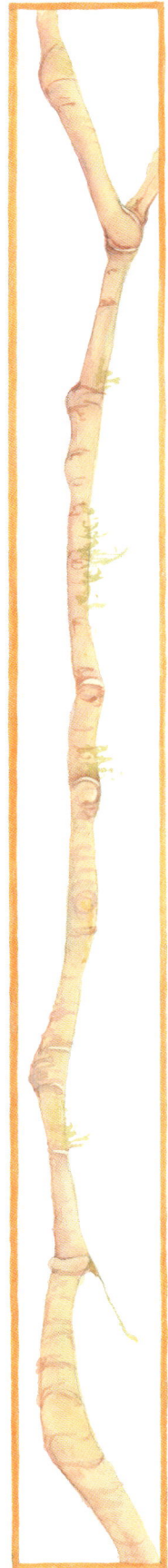

On that day

King Ahasuerus gave to Queen Esther the house of Haman, the enemy of the Jews. And Mordecai came before the king, for Esther had told what he was to her. And the king took off his signet ring, which he had taken from Haman, and gave it to Mordecai. And Esther set Mordecai over the house of Haman.

Then Esther spoke again to the king.

She fell at his feet and wept and pleaded with him to avert the evil plan of Haman the Agagite and the plot that he had devised against the Jews.

When the king held out the golden scepter to Esther, Esther rose and stood before the king. And she said, "If it please the king, and if I have found favour in his sight, and if the thing seems right before the king, and I am pleasing in his eyes, let an order be written to revoke the letters devised by Haman the Agagite, the son of Hammedatha, which he wrote to destroy the Jews who are in all the provinces of the king. For how can I bear to see the calamity that is coming to my people? Or how can I bear to see the destruction of my kindred?"

Then King Ahasuerus said to Queen Esther and to Mordecai the Jew, "Behold, I have given Esther the house of Haman, and they have hanged him on the gallows, because he intended to lay hands on the Jews. But you may write as you please with regard to the Jews, in the name of the king, and seal it with the king's ring, for an edict written in the name of the king and sealed with the king's ring cannot be revoked."

The king's scribes were summoned at that time, in the third month, which is the month of Sivan, on the twenty-third day. And an edict was written, according to all that Mordecai commanded concerning the Jews, to the satraps and the governors and the officials of the provinces from India to Ethiopia, 127 provinces, to each province in its own script and to each people in its own language, and also to the Jews in their script and their language. And he wrote in the name of King Ahasuerus and sealed it with the king's signet ring.

Then he sent the letters by mounted couriers riding on swift horses that were used in the king's service, bred from the royal stud, saying that *the king allowed the Jews who were in every city to gather and defend their lives, to destroy, to kill, and to annihilate any armed force of any people or province that might attack them, children and women included, and to plunder their goods, on one day throughout all the provinces of King Ahasuerus, on the thirteenth day of the twelfth month, which is the month of Adar.* A copy of what was written was to be issued as a decree in every province, being publicly displayed to all peoples, and the Jews were to be ready on that day to take vengeance on their enemies. So the couriers, mounted on their swift horses that were used in the king's service, rode out hurriedly, urged by the king's command. And the decree was issued in Susa the citadel.

Then Mordecai went out from the presence of the king in royal robes of blue and white, with a great golden crown and a robe of fine linen and purple, and the city of Susa shouted and rejoiced.

The Jews had light and gladness and joy and honour. And in every province and in every city, wherever the king's command and his edict reached, there was gladness and joy among the Jews, a feast and a holiday. And many from the peoples of the country declared themselves Jews, for fear of the Jews had fallen on them.

Now in the twelfth month, which is the month of Adar, on the thirteenth day of the same, when the king's command and edict were about to be carried out, on the very day when the enemies of the Jews hoped to gain the mastery over them, the reverse occurred: the Jews gained mastery over those who hated them.

The Jews gathered in their cities throughout all the provinces of King Ahasuerus to lay hands on those who sought their harm. And no one could stand against them, for the fear of them had fallen on all peoples. All the officials of the provinces and the satraps and the governors and the royal agents also helped the Jews, for the fear of Mordecai had fallen on them. For Mordecai was great in the king's house, and his fame spread throughout all the provinces, for the man Mordecai grew more and more powerful.

The Jews struck all their enemies with the sword, killing and destroying them, and did as they pleased to those who hated them. In Susa the citadel itself the Jews killed and destroyed 500 men, and also killed Parshandatha and Dalphon and Aspatha and Poratha and Adalia and Aridatha and Parmashta and Arisai and Aridai and Vaizatha, the ten sons of Haman the son of Hammedatha, the enemy of the Jews, but they laid no hand on the plunder.

That very day

the number of those killed in Susa the
citadel was reported to the king. And the
king said to Queen Esther, "In Susa the
citadel the Jews have killed and destroyed
500 men and also the ten sons of Haman.
What then have they done in the rest of the
king's provinces! Now what is your wish? It
shall be granted you. And what further is
your request? It shall be fulfilled."

And Esther said, "If it please the king,
let the Jews who are in Susa be allowed
tomorrow also to do according to this
day's edict. And let the ten sons of Haman
be hanged on the gallows." So the king
commanded this to be done. A decree was
issued in Susa, and the ten sons of Haman
were hanged. The Jews who were in Susa
gathered also on the fourteenth day of the
month of Adar and they killed 300 men in
Susa, but they laid no hands on the plunder.

Now the rest of the Jews who were in the
king's provinces also gathered to defend
their lives, and got relief from their enemies
and killed 75,000 of those who hated them,
but they laid no hands on the plunder. This
was on the thirteenth day of the month
of Adar, and on the fourteenth day they
rested and made that a day of feasting and
gladness. But the Jews who were in Susa
gathered on the thirteenth day and on the
fourteenth, and rested on the fifteenth day,
making that a day of feasting and gladness.
Therefore the Jews of the villages, who live
in the rural towns, hold the fourteenth day
of the month of Adar as a day for gladness
and feasting, as a holiday, and as a day on
which they send gifts of food to one another.

And Mordecai recorded these things

and sent letters to all the Jews who were in all the provinces of King Ahasuerus, both near and far, *obliging them to keep the fourteenth day of the month Adar and also the fifteenth day of the same, year by year, as the days on which the Jews got relief from their enemies, and as the month that had been turned for them from sorrow into gladness and from mourning into a holiday; that they should make them days of feasting and gladness, days for sending gifts of food to one another and gifts to the poor.*

So the Jews accepted what they had started to do, and what Mordecai had written to them. *For Haman the Agagite, the son of Hammedatha, the enemy of all the Jews, had plotted against the Jews to destroy them, and had cast Pur (that is, cast lots), to crush and to destroy them. But when it came before the king, he gave orders in writing that his evil plan that he had devised against the Jews should return on his own head, and that he and his sons should be hanged on the gallows. Therefore they called these days Purim, after the term Pur.*

Therefore, because of all that was written in this letter, and of what they had faced in this matter, and of what had happened to them, the Jews firmly obligated themselves and their offspring and all who joined them, that without fail they would keep these two days according to what was written and at the time appointed every year, that these days should be remembered and kept throughout every generation, in every clan, province, and city, and that these days of Purim should never fall into disuse among the Jews, nor should the commemoration of these days cease among their descendants.

Then Queen Esther, the daughter of Abihail, and Mordecai the Jew gave full written authority, confirming this second letter about Purim. Letters were sent to all the Jews, to the 127 provinces of the kingdom of Ahasuerus, in words of peace and truth, *that these days of Purim should be observed at their appointed seasons, as Mordecai the Jew and Queen Esther obligated them, and as they had obligated themselves and their offspring, with regard to their fasts and their lamenting.* The command of Queen Esther confirmed these practices of Purim, and it was recorded in writing.

King Ahasuerus imposed tax on the land and on the coastlands of the sea. And all the acts of his power and might, and the full account of the high honour of Mordecai, to which the king advanced him, are they not written in the Book of the Chronicles of the kings of Media and Persia? For Mordecai the Jew was second in rank to King Ahasuerus, and he was great among the Jews and popular with the multitude of his brothers, for he sought the welfare of his people and spoke peace to all his people.

Explaining this Esther manuscript

Changes of font in the text

- Section headings are in larger font size with decorative first letter
- Content of edicts are in *italics*
- Subheadings and emphases are in **bold italics**

Notes

- (1) a talent is about 34 kilograms
- (2) a cubit is about 45 centimetres

The illustrations are mostly rainforest motifs (mostly from Sea Acres National Park, Port Macquarie, New South Wales) to suggest decorations fit for a Persian palace

Title Page	Azure kingfisher, *Alcedo azurea* and hanging vine
Pages 86-87	*Left* Hangings for a royal feast: hanging vines and purple fruits (including *Cissus antarctica*, White beech, Lillypilly, Dianella, Black apple, Sandpaper fig, *Ficus coronata*, and Rose maple).
	Right Feather of the superb lyrebird, *Menura novaehollandiae*, to quill the king's edict.
Pages 88-89	Decorations for a Persian king's harem and bride.
	Top border White on blue includes fallen rainforest flowers of the Ebony myrtle, Native olive, White orchid (*Pratia purpuerascens*), and *Backhousia anistata* (*myrtacea* family). Blue and gold on white includes *Plectranthus argentatus*, Native frangipani (*Hymenosporum flavum*), *Myrtella*, *Kreysigia multiflora*, *Orthosiphon aristatus*, Native lilac hibiscus (*Alyogyne huegelli*), *Prostanthora ovalifolia*, and *Thelychiton kingianus* and captive Azure kingfisher.
	Lower border Blue on white is the ground-cover vine known as native wandering Jew *Commelina cyanea*. White and gold on blue are scented flowers including the Bolwarra, Native frangipani, Brush box and Native musk (*Oleavia argophylla*), culminating in the Norfolk Island Wedding lily.
Pages 90-91	*Top* Feather of a Grey butcherbird, *Cracticus torquatus*, to quill Haman's evil edict.
	Lower border Lots cast: Wandering Jew, Butcher bird, hanging vines and cygnet.
Pages 92-93	Death sentence: young Strangler fig taking hold of an Ebony myrtle, bordered by narrow panels of marble, porphyry, kingfisher feathers and Wandering Jew.
Pages 94-95	*Left* Hanging in the air: vines and goanna, *Varamus varius*.
	Right Feast and gallows I: Strangler fig on Ebony myrtle, Myrtella flowers, porphyry, and seeds and nuts including the calyx of Native hibiscus, Native frangipani, *Cleistanthus*, Casuarina, Bolwarra and Macadamia nuts, Maiden's blush, Lemon myrtle and Bangalow palm.
Pages 96-97	*Left* The lofty brought down and the humble raised up: Blue-winged kookaburra, *Dacelo leachii*, Wandering Jew, and Bangalow palm litter.
	Right: Bangalow palm trunk and Blue-winged kookaburra feathers.
Pages 98-99	*Left* Feast and gallows II: one Strangler fig overcome by another, and fruits including Native raspberry and *Aristotelia australasica*, bordered by Myrtella and Kingfisher feathers, figs and Ebony myrtle flowers.
	Right Hanging in the air II.
Pages 100-101	*Top* Blue-winged kookaburra feather to quill Mordecai's edict of defence.
	Lower border Lots countered: cygnet, Azure kingfisher, hanging vines, Lyrebird feather and Blue-winged kookaburra, bordered by Wandering Jew.
Pages 102-103	*Left* Deliverance: azure kingfisher in flight.
	Right Feast after a royal hanging: hanging vines and pale fruits including the Cheese tree, Minchinberry, Silver aspen, *Fieldia australis*, and Lillypilly.
Pages 104-105	Decorations for a Jewish Purim:
	Top border Feather of the Powerful owl *Ninos strenua* to quill Mordecai's letters, and flowers and fruit including the Bootlebrush, Bolwarra, Native raspberry, Lemon myrtle, Silver aspen, *Dendrobium*, and Sandpaper fig. It is edged by a border of flowers including the White orchid, White beech and Native violet.
	Lower borders Lillypillies, White beech, Sandpaper figs, Dianella and Macadamia nuts; and White beech, Myrtle ebony, Bolwarra, Oliver's sassafras, *Cassine australe* and Bootlebrush.
	Dividing the text on the right Esther's seal.

Comment

Reading Esther evoked the lush, rank headiness of rainforest: the heavily scented Bolwarra flowers, the improbable purple fruits of the White beech, the slowly murderous Strangler fig and the rustle of wildlife. I wanted to reflect my response in the border designs as if they were wall decorations in the Persian palace in which the story is set. It opens with a gushy description of a royal feast in purples and golds, marble and porphyry.

Structured around feasts and hangings, the story explores the great biblical themes of deliverance and reversal, and wisdom and folly, with ruthless satire. It could be Esther singing Hannah's song in 1 Samuel 2, or Mary's in Luke 2. My border illustrations suggest these motifs and themes, and the book's symmetrical form centred in the happenstances of chapter 6.

Although I doubt the scribes in the story used them, I draw feathers as if quills suggest the character of each edict or its author. The Lyrebird parades his tail feathers as he sings and dances his courting ritual. The Butcherbird also sings melodiously – but hangs its prey in the forks of trees. The shy Azure kingfisher is royally coloured, cousin to the sturdier Blue-winged kookaburra, with its derisive laugh and posture. The cygnet is simply a bad pun, as one commentator suggests that Haman may have tricked the king into an edict to kill, rather than dispossess, the Jews. Transforming Mordecai from the Kookaburra to the Powerful owl in the last panel suggests his change of status, and provides a visual parallel to the Lyrebird feather of the first.

The goanna I saw in the undergrowth reminded me both of the reptilian Haman and the formation of the Strangler fig I was sketching. Esther's Hebrew name means "Myrtle" – and thus the Strangler fig is attacking the Ebony myrtle, and other myrtle flowers appear in the illustrations. It may also mean "hidden", another theme in the book. I suggest you explore all the book's themes and contrasts of characters (seen and unseen) and their consequences. The Azure kingfisher is subdued and captive in the second panel, and unfettered and free in the second last. The third panel is in mourning colours, and is both reminiscent of designs discovered on Persian ruins from Susa and suggestive of dice used as lots. Its counterpart (panel 8) breaks free of its boundaries and colour scheme. The edicts are in italics, inviting you to carefully compare them. The Bangalow palm leaves in panel 6 suggest the honouring of Mordecai, as the crowds honoured Jesus in Mark 11.

Not all the visual subjects are from the rainforest. The marble and porphyry specimens I sketched in the Australian Museum in Sydney were mined near Bathurst in central NSW. The Hibiscus I chose for its colour comes from South Australia, and the Wedding lily for its name, from Norfolk Island.

National Library of Australia Cataloguing-in-Publication Data

The Scrolls Illuminated:
*An illuminating presentation of The Song of Songs, Ruth,
Lamentations, Ecclesiastes and Esther from the Bible*
ISBN 978-0-646-54720-6
Religion and Theology

Printed in Malaysia by Tien Wah Press (Pte) Ltd

Design assistance: Jeremy Ward and Darren Lever

Distributed by The Bible Society in Australia

With thanks to Andrew & Barbara Podger & Margo Sietsma
whose generosity realised this book's publication.